FULL COURT FAITH

How We Can Be
Used by God for His Good
and Perfect Purpose

GEORGE SHINN
with Don Yaeger

Published by Maxwell Leadership Publishing, an imprint of Forefront Books, Nashville,
Tennessee.
Distributed by Simon & Schuster.

Library of Congress Control Number: 2024925003

Print ISBN: 979-8-88710-016-6
E-book ISBN: 979-8-88710-017-3

Cover Design by Bruce Gore, Gore Studio, Inc.
Interior Design by Bill Kersey, KerseyGraphics

Printed in the United States of America

To my incredible wife,

Megan Shinn.

GOD put her in my life at a critical time,

and she has been a tremendous source of strength,

support, and love!

She walks the walk!

Next to JESUS, she's been the light of my life!

Contents

Foreword by Franklin Graham . . . . · 7

Chapter 1: God's Plans Are Too Big to Fail 9

Chapter 2: My Mother, My Hero 21

Chapter 3: God Turns Our Worst into His Best 33

Chapter 4: God Knows the Way 43

Chapter 5: Trusting God and Dreaming Big 53

Chapter 6: You Can't Outwork Your Need for God 65

Chapter 7: My New Chairman of the Board 75

Chapter 8: God-Sized Growth 85

Chapter 9: Taking Pro Sports for a Test Drive 97

Chapter 10: My Hail Mary from Half Court 109

Chapter 11: God's Slam Dunk for Charlotte 121

Chapter 12: God's Pieces Come Together 137

Chapter 13: Dying for a Win 149

Chapter 14: Building a Winning Team—On *and* Off the Court. 161

Chapter 15: Pride Cometh Before the Fall 173

Chapter 16: Dust and Ashes 185

Chapter 17: A Fresh Start and Historic Tragedy 195

Chapter 18: A Different Kind of Rebuilding Year 205

Chapter 19: Starting a New Season 217

Chapter 20: Finding My True Purpose 229

Acknowledgments 239

Foreword

BY FRANKLIN GRAHAM

When you read the first line of this book, you'll know that George Shinn is a man, in his own words deeply flawed—but has learned that God loves him and can use him in spite of those flaws.

George Shinn is also a friend of mine. As a boy from Kannapolis, North Carolina, he was captured by the automobiles that rolled into his father's service station, never realizing that he would someday have his own sizeable car collection and auction many for charitable causes.

As a young man, defeating voices told him he had no sales ability, yet he went on to excel as a business owner, eventually creating and owning the Charlotte Hornets, bringing the National Basketball Association (NBA) to his home state. He experienced the fruits of his labors—his team attracting great crowds—and led a savvy merchandising campaign. George has packed a lifetime of experiences into eight decades running in the fast lane, facing and succumbing to temptation, overcoming trials, and realizing that through repentance God would still use his life to make a difference for others. That's a full-court shot!

So it should be no surprise that George's life changed while behind the wheel of a car. When he pulled off the road one day overcome by despair, he knew he had to get out of the driver's seat of his life and let God change his heart and his thinking. George made Jesus the CEO of his dreams. Though not always obedient, through his struggles, sin, and brokenness, he realized that God can use the least to accomplish His best.

Great stories are about real people, real challenges, real disappointments, and real transformation. Everyone is on a journey. Everyone has a destination. What is yours? You may see something of yourself in George Shinn. In a sense, life is lived in an arena and we all have the chance to make a difference for the better.

George Shinn is sharing his story—the thrill of action on the court, the horrors of humiliation in the court of law, and the realization that God will take it all and shape people's "full court faith."

"Enter into His courts with praise. Be thankful to Him, and bless His name" (Psalm 100:4).

Franklin Graham,
President & CEO
Billy Graham Evangelistic Association,
Charlotte, North Carolina
Samaritan's Purse, Boone, North Carolina
July 2024

CHAPTER 1
God's Plans Are Too Big to Fail

My name is George, and I am a man.

Being a man also means I'm a few other things. First and foremost, it means I am made in the image of God, and for that I am grateful every day. Pursuing a relationship with Him and being shaped by His presence has been the defining journey of my life. I'm here today to share the good news of what a relationship with God through His Son, Jesus Christ, can do in your life and to encourage you to pursue that loving relationship for yourself.

God has done some amazing things in my life. He changed me from a poor, small-town, North Carolina country boy who almost lost his childhood home into a successful businessman who was able to achieve unbelievable professional goals.

God grew me from the student with the lowest grades in high school into the owner of an empire of business schools. He led me out of mockery as the "poor boy" on the free lunch program at school into experiencing the joy of bringing a National Basketball Association (NBA) expansion franchise, the Charlotte Hornets, to my home state.

God is always incredibly good. We can see how good He is by how much He accomplishes with how little He has to work with.

By that, I mean us.

Being a man also means I am human. Humans, as the Bible reminds us over and over again, are broken.

Literally everyone in the Bible not named Jesus was a sinner. Despite their sins, God used these flawed people to accomplish His plan. God also put them in the Bible to help us learn that, regardless of our shortcomings, He still loves us, wants a relationship with us, and will use us according to His will.

And trust me, I am no different.

God has done many wonderful things in my life—but the biggest things aren't the accomplishments I used to take the most pride in.

Despite my educational shortcomings, I have been extremely blessed in life and business. When no major college would accept me after my admittedly underwhelming high school career, I enrolled in a two-year business college. At first, I was disappointed that I did not have better options, like my many friends who were going off to bigger, more established universities in North Carolina. But I soon realized that God had brought me down this road for a reason.

I was so impressed with the school and what I thought God was showing me by being there that I later bought it and others like it. I eventually owned dozens of these schools and built a business empire from them.

By the mid-1980s, I was wealthy, happily married, and able to accomplish an impossible dream: bringing a professional sports franchise to Charlotte.

Backed by a group of three investors, I was the face of our effort to bring something special to my town. In some ways, I was the face of the town itself. We had discussions with Major League Baseball, which looked at our population of 350,000 and said we were at least twenty years away from getting a professional team.

I was forty-five at the time, and if I was going to own a professional sports team, I wanted to do it while I was young enough to enjoy it, not when I was in retirement.

Luckily, there were other sports.

Despite its relatively small size compared to other major cities, Charlotte, North Carolina, was the center of many well-known college basketball teams like Duke, the University of North Carolina, North Carolina State, and other Atlantic Coast Conference (ACC) schools.

In the 1980s, Charlotte was one of the fastest-growing cities in the country, with emerging financial industries reflecting the country's economic growth at the time. It was also a time of extreme growth for the NBA, with players like Magic Johnson and Larry Bird, plus North Carolina's own Michael Jordan, helping the league reach unprecedented levels of national and even global attention.

By 1986, the league was officially interested in expanding—and I wanted an NBA team. But we weren't the only city asking for one.

The state of Florida had three cities interested in pursuing an NBA team, including Miami and Orlando. These cities offered fierce competition. I mean, who could compete with Disney?

Minneapolis, which was geographically closer to more established NBA cities, was also submitting a bid.

But on April 3, 1987, in what the *New York Times* called "a surprise move," the NBA awarded its first expansion slot to the city of Charlotte.

It wasn't just a surprise; it was a God-sized miracle. I can now see how God put people in my life and a desire in my heart to make Charlotte's dream a reality. God continued to bless our team and mission for a long time.

God's plan for my life was so much bigger than that, but I had to go through a season of struggle to see it. You've probably heard the phrase, "Growth doesn't happen on the mountaintop; it happens in the valley." That's true in the real world. There's a reason the tops of mountains are bare. Nothing can grow on them. The conditions are too harsh, and the soil is too sparing. It's true in our spiritual lives as well. When we get to the top of whatever our mountain is, whether it's finally getting the promotion we were hoping for or buying our dream car or home, our eyes can start turning away from God.

Owning the Charlotte Hornets and earning the acclaim of my community had that effect on me. I became the toast of the town—but when you're celebrated like that, it's easy to forget who should really get the credit. I started to think my success was about me instead of God. Of course, when you make it about yourself, you're bound to fail.

And boy, did I fail—just not immediately.

For the next decade, our team and my life seemed like something out of a fairy tale.

Our bid for a team drew criticism over the fact that Charlotte's arena was too big. Detractors said we wouldn't be able to sell enough season tickets to keep our arena—with a seating capacity of over twenty-four thousand—filled. But reality proved different. During the first seven seasons of our franchise, we led the NBA in attendance, selling out almost every game. And the team, with our fashionable teal jerseys and fun players, had just as much success on the court as the organization had off the court.

But in 1997, things off the court came crashing down.

I was accused of sexual misconduct in a very public way. While no criminal charges were filed, I was forced to talk about my own failings and indiscretions in a civil trial that was broadcast across the nation.

As publicly as I was celebrated when I brought the Hornets to town, I was just as publicly embarrassed. Even worse, I was privately shunned.

My wife of twenty-seven years filed for divorce. Most of my friends—many of whom I'd been close with for years and never hesitated to help if they needed anything—stopped taking my calls.

As my public reputation cratered, so did support for the team.

We went from leading the league in attendance to not being able to draw enough fans to stay profitable. Things got so bad that I had to move the team to New Orleans, which didn't exactly help my reputation in Charlotte.

A few years after that, I sold the Hornets and walked away.

To the world, my story was over. But to God, it was really just beginning.

God showed me that His loyalty and sovereignty is bigger than my brokenness. As much as we might get it wrong, if we trust in God, He can still make it right.

I know that not only from personal experience. I also know it from what the Bible teaches.

When I was a young boy, I learned the story of Father Abraham and how he had "many sons." As I got older, I learned that Abraham offered an example of profound trust in God as he was prepared to sacrifice his son Isaac out of obedience.

As an adult, I can now see that Abraham's story is much more complex—and much more human.

In the book of Genesis, God made a few different promises to Abraham. First, God told Abraham that He would bless all the families of the earth through his lineage. God also promised Abraham that He would make his descendants more numerous than the stars in the sky and that He would give those descendants a specific land forever, a land where God's family could grow and thrive.

What an amazing promise and blessing! Can you imagine how Abraham must have felt to hear that from God?

But that doesn't mean Abraham got it right all the time after that. Quite the opposite, in fact.

The Bible tells us that, while on their way to the land God promised, Abraham and his wife lived in Egypt for a while because of a famine. Abraham (then named Abram) was afraid that the Egyptians might kill him to take for themselves his beautiful wife, Sarah (then named Sarai). Abram lied to Pharaoh and claimed Sarai was his sister. As a result, Pharaoh treated Abram well and took Sarai into his palace!

But God intervened, saved Sarai and Abram, and allowed them to continue the journey to the land that He had promised.

Yet Abram would still have a hard time trusting God completely after that.

After they reached the land God had led them to, God entered into a covenant with Abram to give his family and all their descendants this amazing land and to give him an heir of his own blood. Abram fulfilled his part of the covenant with a sacrifice of a "heifer, a goat and a ram, each three years old, along with a dove and a young pigeon" (Genesis 15:9).

But in the very next chapter, Abram strayed from God's promise!

Despite the promise God made to give him a son, Abram still decided to act on his own behalf instead of waiting on God.

Because both Abram and Sarai were older, they doubted God's ability to give them a son through childbirth. Their problems seemed too big for God, so they tried to solve the problem themselves.

At his wife's suggestion, Abram slept with Hagar, his wife's handmaid. With Hagar, Abram had a son named Ishmael.

I know what it looks like to be aware of what God has promised—but then still try to get something for myself. Yet, once again, God showed Abram grace.

That's actually a pretty big understatement. God didn't just show him grace but blessed him in ways unlike anyone else. The Bible is full of stories like that. After all, if God didn't use broken sinners, who else would He have?

Look at Moses. Yes, Moses was a sinner before God used him to lead His people to the promised land. Part of what makes God so amazing is how our imperfect lives are redeemed when they are used as part of His perfect story. While we always recognize Moses as a great leader, we often overlook his problems and flaws. Moses was a murderer with a speech impediment. But God used him to deliver the people of Israel from slavery. Moses was also God's vehicle for communicating the Ten Commandments. God did so much in Moses's life! Yet, at the end of the journey, just as he was on the verge of entering the promised land, Moses forgot about God. In chapter 20 of the book of Numbers, we are taught that Moses struck the rock to produce water for his people instead of speaking to it as God had commanded.

As punishment, God kept Moses from entering the promised land.

The point is, Moses was one of the most important men in the Old Testament. But he was a sinner. Even after years of faithfully following God, Moses still had moments of human brokenness, times when he wanted to do things his own way instead of God's way as we see in the incident with the rock. But he's still a part of God's story.

It was no different for Jonah. The Bible tells us God instructed Jonah to go to Nineveh to warn the people to turn away from their wickedness. But instead of being honored that God chose him to carry out this mission, Jonah disagreed with God. Jonah did not think Nineveh deserved the chance to be saved. Even worse, he disobeyed, jumped on a ship, and fled in the opposite direction.

I relate to Jonah. There have been many times when I was given the chance to do something I thought God was calling me to do, but I still found myself walking the wrong way.

That kind of choice has never worked for me.

The good news is that God can handle our failures—all of them, including our inability to trust Him completely. I've definitely failed not only in trusting God but in remembering His greatness. But I thank God for reminding me I'm not the only one to do it. The Bible is full of examples of people who turned away from God but found their way back through His grace. Just as important, these flawed, sinful people became part of God's plan in spite of themselves.

David, the Bible tells us, was "a man after God's own heart." God blessed him, like Abraham and Moses before, in unimaginable ways. Even as a boy, David defeated the incredibly feared Goliath with only a stone and a slingshot. Later, despite David being the youngest and smallest in his family, God made him king. Much later, through David's family line, our true King and Savior, Jesus Christ, was born.

Despite these blessings, David wasn't perfect. Far from it.

The Bible tells us how David, as ruler and king, saw a woman named Bathsheba and was so taken with her that he sent messengers to bring her to him. After meeting her, David slept with her despite the fact that she was married to Uriah, one of his soldiers. David then sent Uriah to the front of the battlefield and gave his commanding general a specific battle plan that ensured Uriah's death in combat.

Not only was Uriah killed but several other men lost their lives because of the foolish way David's general was ordered to fight (2 Samuel 11:22–24). Scripture also makes it clear that, while David would take Bathsheba to be his wife and while she would bear him a son, "the thing David had done displeased the LORD" (2 Samuel 11:27).

I, too, have done things to displease the Lord. I still do every day, though I try not to.

But, as with David, God was good enough to not allow that to be the end of my story.

It certainly wasn't the end of David's.

David didn't let his season of sin define him. After being rebuked by the prophet Nathan, David repented and went about a life of service to God and others, ruling justly as a great king of Israel. But more than anything he did for his earthly kingdom, David ensured his eternal legacy through his contributions to God's kingdom, pointing the nation to God and writing most of the Psalms.

Obviously, I haven't done anything close to that.

But after losing some of the things I thought meant the most to me—namely, my team, my marriage, and the reputation I had in the community—I learned that my story wasn't done. I realized that, while I might have lost so much in the eyes of the world, God still thought I was worthy of being part of His story.

I've long believed that a strong man is one who can build a foundation with the bricks others have thrown at him. Through God's grace, that's what I've spent the last two decades trying to do.

This book is my story to some extent. But, really, it's God's story.

It's the story of how God has blessed me throughout my life. When I was trying to be a good servant, He gave me opportunities to serve. When I was less faithful, He gave me opportunities to grow. And, as I grew, He allowed me opportunities to bless others through His faithfulness.

Now, as I approach Abraham's age when God made him a father for the first time, I can look back and see how much bigger my life is because of God's role in it.

I never allowed my failures to define me. More importantly, neither did God.

And because of God's goodness, my story has continued, and each chapter has brought new reminders of God's ability to use all things for His purpose.

In the pages ahead, I want to share all of it with you—the wins, losses, opportunities, mistakes, and missteps, and how God remained faithful through it all.

None of us are perfect. But with God, through the sacrifice of His Son, Jesus Christ, we are made perfect.

And I'm living proof that when we put God first, despite our imperfections, His plans are too big to fail.

CHAPTER 2
My Mother, My Hero

Looking back, I can see how God equipped me in several ways for the journey I would take. The biggest way He helped me was giving me a mother who prepared me for the challenges I would face in life by being honest about the ones she faced in hers.

Born Irene Sarah Cline, my mother grew up in the small town of Concord, North Carolina. She had a big family, with four kids and her parents, William and Margaret, all living under one roof.

No matter how much money your parents make, splitting it six ways doesn't leave you with too much of it. So, like a lot of people back then, my mother grew up with the necessities but few luxuries. But she learned in the lean times to celebrate the blessings God bestowed on her. Money wasn't her only struggle in life, however; she had also experienced hardship in her relationships, and by the time she met my father, George Shinn, she had already endured a failed marriage.

My dad had endured his share of hardships as well. His first wife had passed away when she was only twenty-eight. Life was more difficult and medical technology wasn't as advanced back then, so such tragedies were more common than they are today.

Of course, that didn't make it any easier for Dad to lose the woman he thought was the love of his life so early. That's the thing about life though: the longer you live, the more perspective you get and the more you can see God's fingerprints on everything in your life, even the things that seemed devastating at the time.

I think that's one of the most important things I've learned about God: it's our job to look back and see the ways He has shaped our lives and used all of it to bring us into His story.

It was a tragedy for my father to lose his first wife, but that's also what enabled him to marry my mom and gave them— united in some way by shared hardship—the opportunity to bring me into this world.

My dad was born and raised in Kannapolis, North Carolina, just north of Charlotte. He and my mother lived there after they were married. Both my parents had children from their first marriages, but my half-siblings were much older by the time I was born in 1941. They named me George Shinn Jr., but growing up, I just went by Junior.

Kannapolis was unique in that it wasn't an incorporated city. It was actually owned by Cannon Mills, a textile manufacturing company that was the largest manufacturer of sheets and towels in the world. As a result, Kannapolis had the nickname of Towel City.

My father was a successful business owner, running the Towel City Service Station, which functioned as something of a hub for local commerce. It was a white brick building with big blue letters on the top spelling out the name.

I spent most of my afternoons sitting outside my father's store, watching all the different cars pull into and out of the gas pumps. I suppose that's where my lifelong love of cars comes from. Boy, were some of them pretty! I think my love for and appreciation of cars began by seeing them come by our store, which was, in part, a Gulf gas station. We also sold groceries, some of which we raised on our family property. Dad also had a pool table inside, and some of the men from town would hang out there shooting pool and sipping on sodas they'd buy. The more pool they played, the more soda they drank—and the more money my dad made.

My father knew something about people that helped him become such a successful businessman. He knew people hate *being sold* something, but they love to *buy* stuff. For example, he didn't have to push his refreshments on customers; he just had to put a pool table in back and offer them the chance to stay as long as they'd like. People bought a lot of soda, gas, and food from Towel City Service Station, and our family was better off as a result.

Not that it wasn't hard work.

My father was one of the hardest workers I knew, and it was clear from an early age that I was expected to be one as well. Even as a young boy, I was put to work at the store, doing odd jobs like taking out the trash and making sure the soda bottles were stocked up. Part of the reason I worked so hard was that I liked doing all the odd jobs around the station. I also wanted to see my dad, which meant I had to be at the store. He worked incredibly long hours.

That's what mattered most to my father—working hard and delivering good value to our customers. If you did that, my dad always said, the results would come. And, for him, they did.

My father was a successful businessman with ambitions to expand beyond the service station. He had an idea he said would dramatically change our family's financial situation.

We were already pretty successful, but my dad was dreaming bigger. He didn't just want to own a neighborhood market; he wanted to own a whole neighborhood! He went to the bank and borrowed the money to get the project started. As collateral, he mortgaged our home and the service station. He purchased the land around our home—a sizable number of acres—for the development and marked off the lots where each home would be located. Running through the whole area was one main road he had built. He named it Irene Avenue, after my mother.

It was an incredibly exciting time. I already felt like I was one of the luckier kids I knew because my dad owned a store and I got to wash fancy cars. But now I could sense that our lives were about to change in even more dramatic ways.

I was right—our lives did change dramatically.

But not for the better.

Shortly after construction began on the development, my father, at the age of fifty, had a stroke.

He had just left the service station and was walking to the bank, carrying with him a little bank bag that contained his daily deposit. But before he made it to the bank, he collapsed on the sidewalk. He was rushed to the hospital, but somehow amid all that activity, the bag of money disappeared.

So did my dad.

My mom went to the hospital while I stayed at the house. My oldest brother, who was much older than me and lived in New Jersey, came down that afternoon. The next day, he took me out to breakfast at a little café called Country Kitchen, which was just across the street from our house and catty-corner from the service station. We sat at the bar and ordered breakfast. He got bacon and eggs, and I got scrambled eggs. I remember he kidded me about asking for ketchup.

"You're messing up your eggs, Junior," he told me. I was a little embarrassed, but I liked my eggs how I liked them.

Then he said something that made me forget about breakfast.

"Daddy," he said with a pause, "has gone to heaven. He's with Jesus now."

I was eight years old.

Years later, my family would discover that he suffered a devastating stroke in the right frontal lobe of his brain. Back then, it didn't really matter. All I knew was that my dad was gone, and with all of my older siblings out of the house, my mother was all on her own.

Some women are the strong, silent type who will suffer things stoically and keep the hurt and pain from the people around them, including their children.

That wasn't Irene Shinn.

My mom was incredibly honest and vulnerable in how she handled her grief. I'll never forget seeing her say goodbye to my father for the last time.

Back then, when someone died, the body would be brought to the home. A wreath would be hung on the door, and friends, neighbors, and family would come by and view the body and pay their respects. That's what we did for my father. I remember seeing his casket sitting there in our home. I was curious about how Daddy could be there in our living room but also be with Jesus in heaven. I was also scared to actually look at the body, so I tried to avoid it.

After all the people had come and gone, the workers from the funeral home told my mother they were ready to take him to the cemetery and needed to close the casket.

"Would you like to see your husband one last time, Mrs. Shinn?" they asked.

"Yes," my mother said through heavy sobs.

My mother reached in, grabbed Daddy's hand, and started praying to God. The tears continued, and her cries grew louder. As she stood up, she grabbed Daddy's hand and then eventually his entire body, just holding him and weeping. She even tried to pull him out of the casket.

My mother was so overcome with grief and despair, the funeral home workers eventually had to pull my mother off his body. It was scary—but it also told me just how much she loved Daddy.

The tears continued after the funeral. She wept openly and frequently, crying out to God in devastation and despair.

I would come to learn that God uses our toughest times to draw us closer to Him. Seasons of struggle are the things we try hardest to avoid and the times we enjoy the least, but they are the ones God uses to do the most.

Our lives were turned completely upside down after Dad died. Suddenly, Mom not only mourned the sudden passing of the man she thought she would grow old with but also had to enter a world she knew very little about. Still grieving every day, she had to run the business . . . or at least try to. Between pumping gas and selling groceries, she had to try to unravel and understand the financial reality my dad had left. We had a successful business, but it, along with our home, was heavily mortgaged. That meant Mom also had to deal with the mountain of debt and the creditors who came around regularly to check on their investments.

Having to take care of all the tasks suddenly thrust on her was helpful in a way. Yes, my dad was gone—but at least she had something to occupy her time and thoughts.

I think it's important to see things in life that way, to see God that way. I learned how to do that from my mom.

My mom struggled and suffered after my father's passing, but she always saw God in all of it.

"Dark days and bad times will come," she often told me, "but remember your source of strength is the courage to get on your knees and ask God for guidance." She didn't just say that—she lived it. I can't tell you how many times I would walk by her room at night and see her on her knees by the bed, praying to God.

The book of James tells us to "count it all joy . . . when you meet trials of various kinds" (James 5:2 ESV). In the wake of my father's passing, we faced lots of trials. While I can't say my mother was joyous in all of them, I can see now how God was glorified in them.

Eventually, the challenges of trying to keep Dad's business and his subdivision development afloat was too much. Our debt was too great, and our resources were too few. It seemed like we would lose everything. Mom's only option was to auction everything off.

I'd like to say that, after losing my dad, losing our material possessions wasn't that big of a deal. But I'd be lying.

When you're eight, your *stuff* matters.

We sold the gas station, the development, all the land it was on, and even our car. I went from being the kid who got to wash fancy cars and could drink soda at my dad's store anytime I wanted to a kid who had to walk everywhere and could barely afford to eat. It was incredibly embarrassing. Mom didn't worry about things like that though. She was too focused on trying to keep us from losing our house.

However, the money we got from selling everything wasn't enough, which meant the bank had to auction off our home.

The auction began, and my mom started bidding. A second bidder jumped in, and the price kept going up—much higher than we thought the house was worth (and much more than my mom could afford).

As it turned out, the second bidder was a neighbor. Once he realized he was bidding against *us*, he backed out of the process. He didn't realize he was costing a widow and her young son more money. But he quit bidding too late, and the price was already steep. My mom won the auction to buy back the house, but our bills had just gone up. A lot.

Once again, though, God would provide.

Colossians 3:23–24 says that "whatever you do, work heartily, as for the Lord and not for men, knowing that from the Lord you will receive the inheritance as your reward. You are serving the Lord Jesus Christ" (ESV).

Because my mom was a willing worker, she had lots of opportunities.

She managed a motel, took jobs working switchboards as a telephone operator, and even worked the checkout counter at the local grocery store.

She did anything and everything she could to make sure that we were okay. In many ways, she reminds me of Jochebed from the Bible.

Many people might not know the name Jochebed, but they're very familiar with her son Moses. When the Egyptians were slaughtering Hebrew boys, Jochebed put her son in a basket and sent him down the river, knowing it was the only way he would survive. After Moses was discovered and adopted by Pharaoh's daughter, God worked it out so that Jochebed became Moses's nurse and helped raise him—all while concealing her true connection to the baby boy.

I can't imagine how hard it must have been for Jochebed to release Moses into that river. She trusted God, though, and He rewarded her faith. God saved Moses's life and put him into an amazing place of power to be trained and educated. God also rewarded Jochebed's faith by bringing her back into Moses's life as his nurse.

Some people might think Jochebed must have suffered, watching her son be raised by another woman. But if you have the correct, God-filtered perspective, you can see the blessings through the challenges.

Jochebed was blessed to still be in Moses's life. The Egyptians had explicitly set out to murder Hebrew boys, but God made a way for her to still raise Moses. God ensured the person He had chosen to lead His people out of slavery would be raised by a godly woman, even in a pagan environment where evil reigned. Being such a godly woman, Jochebed would have appreciated and recognized the way God was working in her and her son's lives.

Irene Shinn, even amid losing her husband and nearly her home, was the same way.

My mother never focused on the negatives; she chose to focus on the blessings. That's not to say she was all sunshine and rainbows. As I said, she wept often as part of the mourning process.

God welcomes our tears.

In the book of Matthew, Jesus told the crowd assembled for His Sermon on the Mount, "Blessed are those who mourn, for they will be comforted" (Matthew 5:4). My mother definitely mourned, but she invited God into that grieving space and, as a result, was comforted. Not only was she blessed by a sense of God's peace in her life but she demonstrated an authentic struggle while still loving God.

I think we as Christians sometimes struggle to reconcile what we see as the good parts of God's blessings with the parts we don't like as much. How can God be good when bad things happen?

My mother taught me that God is in all of it. At all times, whether you are celebrating the groundbreaking of an exciting new business or mourning the sudden loss of a loved one, God is in charge all the time.

Being raised by a woman who taught me those values was one of the greatest blessings I have ever received—and that blessing wouldn't have happened without the loss of my father.

Life without Dad was tough. We didn't have a lot. But the one thing my mother reinforced to me over and over was that, with God, whatever we had was enough.

Looking back, I can see the majesty of God's plan. As I got older, I certainly had many more painful disruptions to my life. I'd lose wives. I'd lose friends. I'd leave my home state.

But I never lost God. More specifically, He never lost me.

Going through my father's death so early and having my mother set such an example—teaching me to be grateful for so little after losing so much—shaped my faith in ways I didn't realize until years later. You can't realize how much growth occurs in the valley until God brings you through it and out the other side.

The Bible doesn't hide the fact that struggle and suffering are absolutely parts of God's plan for our spiritual development.

Growing up as a poor child of a widowed single mother, I would have plenty of developing to do.

CHAPTER 3

God Turns Our Worst into His Best

One thing is clear in the Bible: Even when you think a story is one of sadness and despair, it's never too late for God to turn it around. After He does—sometimes *way* after—you'll usually realize that going through that season of pain played an essential part in God preparing you for whatever He had in store for you next.

Look at the story of Joseph in the book of Genesis.

Born to Jacob and Rachel, Joseph experienced an amazing journey of ups and downs, twists and turns that was wholly orchestrated by God. Children learn the story of Joseph and his colorful coat in Sunday school, but that's just part of the story. The bigger narrative is one of rich meaning and truth that I experienced in my own life.

Joseph was given his coat by his father, Jacob, who loved Joseph more than his other eleven sons. Understandably, Joseph's brothers were jealous of him, which ultimately led them to kidnap him and sell him into slavery. Imagine being Joseph in that moment, betrayed by your own family, separated from your doting father, and headed off to an unknown future in a much worse situation through no fault of your own.

Some people might have gotten down or given up. Not Joseph. It's always easier to trust God when you know God. And Joseph knew God.

Joseph's faith and character allowed him to earn the trust of his master, Potiphar, who was in charge of the Egyptian ruler Pharaoh's guard. Joseph was a slave, but he still shined brightly and excelled at everything he put his hands to. Eventually, Potiphar made him the superintendent of his household. Though still a slave, Joseph earned his master's favor and respect. This favor evaporated the moment Potiphar's wife tried to seduce Joseph, who refused her advances and ran away. The rejected lady of the house then accused Joseph of rape, and Potiphar didn't hesitate to throw him in prison.

For a second time, through no fault of his own, Joseph was taken to a dark place he never wanted to go.

Again excelling at everything he did, Joseph was soon put in charge of the other prisoners. Later, when two of Pharaoh's servants were sent to prison and confounded by their recurring dreams, Joseph interpreted the meaning for them. Years later, after one of the servants had been released from prison and returned to Pharaoh's service, he suggested the king call on Joseph to interpret his own troubling dreams. Joseph was brought before Pharaoh and listened to him describe his unusual and detailed dream, and God gave Joseph the correct interpretation. Pharaoh was so impressed with Joseph that he put the former slave and prisoner in charge of the Egyptian government! Joseph was second only to Pharaoh, and he used his God-given gifts to save Egypt, his own family, and ultimately the nation of Israel by shepherding them through a terrible seven-year famine.

The key is, even in the lowest stages of Joseph's environment, God's presence in Joseph's life was obvious. In fact, that's really why Pharaoh decided to take Joseph out of prison. It wasn't because of Joseph; it was because of what God was doing *through* Joseph. God was the reason Joseph was elevated. Even someone like Pharaoh, who didn't love or know God, could see it.

Like Joseph's, both my life and my mother's life were dramatically altered, through no fault of our own. We went from being privileged and envied to being pitied and ridiculed. But my mom never let any of this impact her relationship with God. She never let it keep people from seeing God's strength in her own weakness.

She was much better at it than me.

As a boy, I still remembered the things we used to have before my father died. At times, I would be envious of the things I saw my friends have that we didn't. Mom never let me dwell on it though. She often went out of her way to make me appreciate the things we did have.

One day, I was at a friend's house after school, and his parents invited me to stay for dinner. I knew my mother was home making dinner for me at that moment. Even though we ate very modest meals, I still wanted to go home and eat with my mother. So, I politely declined the invitation. When I headed out the door, though, I noticed my friend and his parents were sitting down to a steak dinner.

Now, I'd never had a steak in my life. Honestly, just the smell of those steaks made my mouth water. Suddenly, I was less enthusiastic about heading home to what was waiting.

When I got home for dinner, I smelled a different aroma. Mom was making hamburgers.

As much as I loved my mother and tried to appreciate how hard she worked to provide for me as a single parent, I snapped.

"Mom, guess what the Torrances are having for dinner tonight? Real steaks. We have to have hamburgers."

I know my mom could sense how disappointed I was—not just with that night's dinner but with what that dinner represented. She knew just what to say.

"Don't feel bad for them, Junior," she said.

Wait. Why would *I* feel bad for *them*?

"Steak is just beef," she continued. "Like these hamburgers or the meatloaf we have on Sundays. Maybe the Torrances can't afford to have their beef ground up."

I can see how silly—and how sweet—it was for my mother to say that. But it made sense to me, so I believed her. As a result, I stopped feeling sorry for myself, and I appreciated what we had.

It worked for a while at least. Eventually, my mother couldn't hide from me what our economic reality had become.

The other kids in school made sure of it.

Today, food stamps and welfare come on a government-issued credit card. There are a couple of reasons for this, but one of the main reasons is to make it less obvious who is using government assistance. Back then, it wasn't as easy to hide. On occasion, my mother and I would receive government handouts. I wore hand-me-down clothes from other families at our church. I also got free lunches at school. This was a lot less common back then, and it carried with it an extremely negative social stigma, especially in the eyes of my classmates. No one wanted to be the poor kid in school, and I did my best not to look or act poor. There was a girl in our class who received free lunch. She often came to school so dirty that our teachers would help her bathe in the school bathroom. No one had to help keep me clean.

One day, though, my secret was revealed in the most embarrassing way. I had a crush on the prettiest, smartest girl in school. We considered ourselves boyfriend and girlfriend—at least by fifth-grade standards.

Because she was the smartest person in the class, she was in charge of collecting the lunch money from all the students. On one particular day I seemed to have irritated her. I can't remember what I did to make her so mad, but to get even with me, when the teacher asked her if she had collected everyone's lunch money, she loudly declared, "Yes ma'am! There are twenty-eight paid lunches, and two free lunches."

There was a pause. I knew I was in trouble. She said the name of the girl and then smiled before adding, "And George Shinn!"

Everyone in the classroom turned and fixed their eyes on me. Sure, everyone knew the dirty girl was poor. Now they knew about me. It was one of the most humiliating moments of my youth. But things would get worse.

Now that my secret was out, the other kids in my class, as fifth graders are prone to do, ridiculed me mercilessly. Everywhere I went, I was greeted with chants of "Poor Boy."

That experience shaped me in some key ways. I was so embarrassed that I made a promise to myself: I would never treat people the way the kids in my school had treated me. I would make it a point to go out of my way to be nice and to try and help people that, for whatever reason, were from disadvantaged backgrounds. I never looked at the dirty girl the same way again. No matter how I dressed, we were the same. She deserved my help, not my pity.

The other thing I promised myself was that I never wanted to feel that way again. Whatever it took, I had to be successful. Whatever job I had to take to make money, I would do my best in it. However long I had to work, I would. I would not be made fun of for being poor again.

For her part, my mom told me not to pay attention to the taunts of the other kids. She said you can't control what other people say or think, but you can control two things that will help make you successful: trust God and work your tail off.

I was working on trusting God, but one thing I never struggled with was working hard—even if it didn't always have the best result.

After my dad passed, my mom tried as hard as she could to keep the service station running. I worked there with her, doing anything I could to help.

One day, a man came in with his elderly mother. He drove a Ford Coupe and asked me to wash it—but he had one condition.

"Make sure you do a good job on those windows," he warned. "I want them to be so clean it looks like the windows are down even when they aren't."

The 1949 Ford Coupe was a beautiful car, and I wanted to keep it looking so.

I can remember really taking more time and putting extra effort to make sure, after the car was washed, that no streaks or spots were left on the windows. I went over the windows a third time with my towel just to be sure, finally convinced it was up to the man's standard.

When I was done, the man and his mother got back into the car.

Now, at the time, a popular habit among adults of all ages was to use chewing tobacco, or "dipping snuff." This was especially true in North Carolina back in the 1950s. They don't call stretches of North Carolina "Tobacco Road" for nothing.

Well, the man's mother was also a fan of dipping snuff. When she went to spit the tobacco juice out the window, she either forgot to roll it down or couldn't tell that it was rolled up. She spit a big wad of snuff right onto the window, leaving a mess all over my newly cleaned masterpiece. The tobacco dripped all over the inside of the door.

The man and his mother were embarrassed. I took it as a sign I had done an excellent job on the windows. To his credit, the man wasn't mad at me. How could he be? He just told me to please clean it up, and then gave me a one-dollar tip, which, at the time, was a big deal.

I was appreciative of the gesture, which taught me that if you really work hard at something, financial reward can follow.

But even with that relative windfall, our financial situation was still pretty bleak. My mom was working many jobs, and she was truly trying her best. But for a woman on her own without any formal training on how to run a business, it was too much. I was frustrated because I wanted to help, but I was too young. I could tell she was struggling. It was a hard time, and I would, on occasion, take out some frustration on my mom.

I was especially mad one night. As a growing boy who was feeling like he was emerging as the man of the house, I felt rebellious. When my mother wouldn't give me my way on something, I got so angry that I told her I was going to run away from home.

"Okay, if that's what you want to do," she said. "But I'll miss you."

I wanted her to miss me. That was the point! So, I headed off in a huff.

I didn't get very far. I went to my friend's house and stayed there as long as I could—or at least long enough to make my mom begin to worry about me. When I was sure she was just pacing around our house in worry and had learned *her* lesson, I decided to do her a favor and head back to the house.

I got back to the house expecting her to be waiting on the front step or, better yet, to run toward me like the father did in the Bible story of the prodigal son.

Instead, not only was she not on the front step; she wasn't outside at all. When I got to the front door, it was locked. *This can't be right*, I thought.

I went around to the back door, but that was also locked. Confused, I started banging on my mother's window. Maybe something was wrong with her. It didn't make any sense.

I continued circling the house, calling my mother's name, but got no response. I started to get worried, until I got back around to the front of the house and noticed on the front porch a small paper bag with my name on it. Inside, I saw two sandwiches, along with a note that read, "I just wanted to pack you something since you are leaving. I still love you. Goodbye, Mom."

I grabbed my sandwiches and headed back to my friend's house. By the time I got there, he said I couldn't stay with him. I ended up sleeping on a chair on his porch. When I woke up, I walked back to my house and tried the door again. This time, it was open, and my mother was in the kitchen. When I walked in, I saw she had made me breakfast, and a plate was set out for me at the table. I started to tear up, knowing I had made a mistake and thankful for the grace my mom displayed by forgiving me and showing me mercy.

That was the best thing about my mom. She didn't just talk to me about the Bible and God. She lived out biblical truths in a real way. She lived those truths because of the examples she learned from the Bible.

The grace she showed me is exemplified time and again in the story of God's love for us. Even when we mess up, God's love for us is bigger than our disobedience and rebellion.

My mom's love for me was big enough to handle me running away. In the Bible, Joseph's love for his family was bigger than the hatred from his brothers, even when they sold him into slavery.

When Joseph proved that God had given him the power to interpret dreams, Pharaoh was smart enough to listen. Joseph told Pharaoh there would be seven years of harvest, followed by seven years of famine. Pharaoh put Joseph in charge of the plans to make sure enough food was saved during the years of plenty to endure the leaner times.

But not everyone prepared so well. Joseph's brothers back in Canaan eventually ran out of food and were sent to Egypt by their father to beg for assistance.

Joseph disguised himself from them at first. He even taught them a little lesson, much like my mother did to me when I ran away. But Joseph was eventually so overcome with emotion that he wept and forgave them. Actually, he didn't just forgive them. The Bible tells us he "restored" them. He gave his brothers bountiful provisions for them to take home to his father, and eventually his entire family moved to Egypt. That was how Israelites came to live in Egypt.

The rebellion of Joseph's brothers became part of more than just his story; it became part of God's story. God took their hatred and jealousy and used it to elevate not just one person but *all* His chosen people. That's how great our God is: *He can use our worst to accomplish His best.*

The good news for me was, even though times were hard for me and mom, my story and journey with God was just beginning. While I didn't know it at the time, I was going to have a lot more chances to experience God in some amazing ways—because I had plenty of struggles still to come.

CHAPTER 4
God Knows the Way

One of the reasons it has become easy to trust God is that, both in terms of what I've seen in my life and in the lives of people I read about in the Bible, I know God will always prevail. No matter how much we try to rebel or reject God's love and plan for our lives, He wins. Joseph's brothers sold him into slavery, which saw him forcefully moved to another country. That was not a problem for God. He just used that as an opportunity for Moses to glorify God by leading His people back to the promised land.

When God sent Jesus to earth as a demonstration of His unrelenting love for us as people, we didn't just reject it. The people on earth beat, tortured, and publicly executed Jesus. But it didn't stop God's plan. He just used that as an opportunity to show how God's love for us transcends even the physical limitations of life and death. While the Roman Empire that presided over Jesus's death is no more, Christianity remains. The story of God's church reminds me of Jonah. Jonah ended up where he was supposed to be, even though he didn't see how he would get there at the time.

I can identify with that at a deep and personal level. There have been times when I've turned away from God because I was more interested in pursuing my own interests than His. But God, because His greatness is bigger than my brokenness, kept bringing me back to where He wanted me to be. Sometimes when I speak, I tell the stories of how God has done this in my life and often get choked up. Even after all these years, I am overwhelmed by the sense of God's vast sovereignty. That's the real message of Jonah.

Many children learn the story of Jonah in Sunday school. Ask most of them who are paying attention about Jonah, and they will say, "Jonah was swallowed by a whale!" with some genuine awe and enthusiasm. As an adult, I know the story of Jonah is much richer and more meaningful than that.

As a prophet in Old Testament Israel, Jonah was instructed by God to go to the town of Nineveh and warn the people who lived there that they should repent of their wicked ways and worship God. But the Bible tells us that Jonah, instead of trusting God, ran the other way. He got on a ship headed in the opposite direction from Nineveh.

Of course, that didn't stop God from making sure Jonah ended up where He wanted him to go.

As soon as the ship set off, a big storm with massive waves came, rocking the boat from side to side and stopping it from heading in its intended direction. While the men on the ship were afraid, Jonah knew what God was doing. Jonah was, after all, a prophet.

So, Jonah told them that the high seas were his fault, and if they threw him overboard, their troubles would be over. Knowing Jonah was a man of God, they were afraid to send him to a watery grave but did as he instructed. After throwing Jonah overboard, the seas calmed and "a giant fish" came and swallowed him whole. The Bible tells us Jonah remained in the belly of the giant fish for three days and three nights before being delivered to Nineveh, where God wanted him to go all along.

Now, obviously, there are some parallels to Jesus's story. Jonah was "buried" for three days inside the fish and then "rose" from inside the "tomb" of the belly. In fact, in the New Testament, Jesus even promised people that He would show them "the sign of the prophet Jonah" (Matthew 12:39).

Jonah's story resonates with me because, in addition to it being a sign in the Old Testament that points toward Jesus, I know firsthand what it looks like to start out in one direction only to find yourself in another city and unable to explain how you got there except by God's hand. I see this especially in my career path. I might have ended up as the owner of a large group of business colleges, but I sure didn't start out as any kind of educational superstar. Far from it.

Because I was poor and made fun of by my classmates, I was shy. Add to that the fact that I had a pretty bad stuttering problem as a child. As a result, I hated being called on in class. This fear of participating led to a larger sense of disengagement. I fell behind academically, and if it hadn't been for the help of one of my teachers, I might have been held back a year. Just like God gave Moses his brother, Aaron, to help him with his speech problem, God gave me Mrs. Drummond to help with mine.

Mrs. Drummond was the wife of the school principal. She was one of the sweetest ladies in the state of North Carolina. She saw my potential, but she also saw how my stutter was impacting my performance in school. It hurt my confidence and, as a result, I wasn't as engaged as I could have been. She worked with me every day and taught me to be comfortable and confident in using my words. Slowly but surely, because of her time, attention, and love, I overcame my stuttering. She really was a gift from God.

With my stuttering problem cured, I cautiously began to emerge socially and even got over my fear of public speaking. In fact, I became quite comfortable with it—maybe too comfortable. Because of my quick wit, sense of humor, and a newfound willingness to speak out in class, I became the class clown. As a result, I made many friends and became pretty popular.

Still, I wasn't a strong student. In fact, I barely graduated. The rumor was that I finished dead last in my graduating class. It very well may have been true.

Talk about God using "the least of these."

When you finish last in your class and can't afford college tuition (at least in those days), you don't really have many options once school is over. I can think of only two: You can join the military or you can go and get a job. At five feet six and 135 pounds, I didn't think I would make a very good soldier. Plus, my mother needed me around to help earn money and pay the bills.

She often told me, "If you believe in God and pray and work your tail off, anything can happen." It was time for me to put those words of wisdom to the test. I had already been praying. Now, with school over, the only other thing to do was get to work. I set out to get a job—*any* job.

I still loved cars, and I missed getting to work with them at my dad's old service station, so I took a job at a car wash place. That job showed me I was willing to put in whatever hard work was required if a paycheck was on the line, even if I was doing a job no one else wanted to do. From there, I moved on to where so many people in the Towel City area did: the mill.

I got a job with my buddy Glenn Compton working for the Cannon Mills textile plant in Kannapolis, where my dad's service station had been.

At over six feet tall with a strong build, Glenn was tailor-made for the kind of physical, labor-intensive work we were doing at the mill. We basically had to haul all the fabric from one end of the mill to the other, feeding the machines that would then make the sheets, linens, and, of course, towels that gave Kannapolis the nickname Towel City.

It was pretty basic, mindless stuff. I didn't mind, though, because Glenn and I were doing it together. We spent most of our shifts talking about cars, sports, and/or girls. As much as I enjoyed those worktime conversations with Glenn, it's what I heard from the other employees I worked with that most stood out.

The people who worked at the textile mill were like me in that they never were much for school. Some of them hadn't even finished high school, and those who had certainly hadn't thought about college. But I noticed that whereas I was still trying to figure out what I wanted out of life and how to get it, the people I was working with seemed to feel condemned to the mill for the rest of their lives. They were dissatisfied with what they were getting, but they didn't want to do anything to improve their situations.

Hearing my colleagues in the mill complain about their jobs and other parts of their lives made me curious. I'd ask, "If you don't like what's happening in your life, or if you don't like this job, why don't you try to fix it or change jobs?" I wasn't judging them; I was honestly confused why someone would assume what they have *today* is all they'll *ever* have.

I'm not sure how much the older, veteran employees liked having their life choices questioned by a young kid with a short personality and a big mouth.

Basically, they all thought working at the mill was the best they could do. I didn't agree, but it was a valuable lesson about the mindset of people who seem "stuck" where they are.

Before long, I figured out that working at the mill was *not* the best I could do. Simply put, I couldn't do it anymore.

My job at the mill was physically demanding. I was small, but having worked manual labor jobs most of my life, I felt like I could handle it. Over time, my back disagreed. I eventually developed significant pain between my shoulder blades. At first I sought help from a chiropractor. When that didn't work, I went to see a back specialist. I was told that I had curvature of the spine. If I didn't find a line of work that was less taxing physically, my back would only get worse.

I was disappointed because I liked working with Glenn. But unlike the people I worked with, I was now getting a chance to see what else I might do with my life.

Glenn had an idea.

"George, you like talking to people, and you're good at persuading them," he said. "Why don't you try sales?"

So, Glenn and I took off on an adventure to find a sales job. But what would I sell?

I looked at the want ads in the newspaper, and we drove around town looking at different buildings. When we passed an insurance agency, I thought I had found my next career.

Everyone needs insurance, I thought. I know my mother and I learned the importance of insurance when my father suddenly passed away. I didn't know if the insurance company was hiring, but that didn't stop me from putting on my best clothes and going down the next day to apply.

A man in his midforties greeted me in the office and handed me an application. After I filled it out, I was given a psychological profile test as well. This was a little odd since I had never taken a test like this before. Of course, I hadn't been that good at tests in school, but I did my best and handed it in.

The man took me into a back room and then started grading the test, which apparently was intended to highlight my strengths and weaknesses based on a chart he had on his desk. I watched him stare intently at the scoring rubric, and then back at my test, with a concerned frown across his face.

After a few minutes, he looked up at me and made an effort at one of those half smiles that quickly disappears and falls into a look of severity.

"Mr. Shinn . . ." he began, as his voice trailed off. "I'm sorry. But we won't be able to offer you a job here."

I knew I had never been very good at tests, but I didn't understand how anything on that paper on the man's desk could indicate I was completely unemployable.

"I'm sorry," I protested. "I thought you were hiring."

"Mr. Shinn, there's nothing I can do for you," he told me. "Your test shows you have no sales ability whatsoever. I'm afraid you'll never be able to sell insurance."

Now I wasn't confused. I was angry. Who was this man to tell me what I could or couldn't do?

"Well sir, I appreciate your honesty," I said calmly. "But just so you know, one day I hope to own my own insurance company."

I started walking for the door. I never turned around, but I definitely saw—and still remember to this day—that the man's mouth was wide open as I left.

I was angry, but I was also disappointed. I thought my hurting back would be a way, maybe even God's way, of pushing me where He wanted me to be. I really thought I would be a good insurance salesman. I thought I would be good in a professional setting, even though I hadn't done well in school and, up until that point, had only worked manual labor jobs.

Frustrated and still dealing with an aching back, I had no choice but to return to the mill to continue earning money. My back continued to get worse and so did my attitude.

One night, sensing my despair, my mother said something I found to be fairly amusing at the time.

"Junior," she began innocently, "do you think you could use some more education?"

Always sarcastic, I said, "Well sure, Mom. I could use a lot more education. But where am I going to get it?"

"Why not go to college?" she asked.

I have to admit, I've always loved and respected my mother. But at that moment I did not think she was making any sense.

"College?!" I repeated in disbelief. "You *do* remember that I wasn't a good student? Plus, how would we afford it? I definitely wouldn't get any scholarships. Besides, I'm way too old to be going back to school."

"That's not true," my mother calmly replied. "A lot of veterans are now going back to school, and they are older than you. And if you want to get a job that won't be so hard on your back, you will probably be in some kind of business office." Then she said it: "Why not go to business college?"

Sometimes you can look back at moments in your life and know how important they are. The moments when you knew you were headed in the right direction. The moments when you knew things were supposed to happen. The moments when you sensed your life was changing for the better.

This was not one of those moments. I still thought my mom's idea was crazy.

"Business college!" I exclaimed. "Mother, those are for girls who want to become secretaries."

"No, they aren't," she said gently. "The Harrison boy who just graduated from high school is starting at the business college."

"Oh? Does he want to become a secretary?"

"No, silly. He's going to take over his family's department store business one day, and so he wants to learn about business administration."

In that moment, I realized that even though I wasn't working at the mill right that second, I might as well have been lugging fabric from one machine to another. I sounded just like all the people who hated being in the mill but refused to do anything about it. Here my mother was trying to give me a way out, and I kept arguing about why I shouldn't take it.

I decided to stop arguing with my mother and think about it. I had to admit, it was intriguing. As always, my mother was right. If I didn't want to keep doing manual labor, I needed to figure out something else.

I thought about it that night and talked to my buddy Glenn the next day. He thought it was a good idea, though he had a question.

"How much is tuition?" he asked.

"I don't know," I admitted. "I'm not really sure what I can afford, anyway."

"Well, maybe it won't be so bad. You won't know until you check it out."

Like my mother, he was right. The same advice I had offered to the people I worked with at the mill was now being offered to me: "If you don't like your circumstances, why don't you change them?"

The next day, I did. I made the twenty-mile drive south to Concord and walked into the front door of Evans Business School to meet with the director.

I walked into that door a young, broke millworker with a bad back and not much education. I had no idea how much God would change my circumstances in that school.

CHAPTER 5

Trusting God and Dreaming Big

One of the elements of the story of Jonah that often gets overlooked is what happened to the men who were on the ship with him. At first they tried to row back to shore, but the conditions in the sea were too strong. God is always too strong.

Once they realized they couldn't go their own way, they threw Jonah overboard. We always focus on the fact that Jonah was swallowed by the great fish. But don't forget, as the Bible tells us, once the men threw Jonah overboard and the seas became calm again, they recognized the power of the Lord. Jonah 1:16 says that when the storm stopped, "the men greatly feared the LORD, and they offered a sacrifice to the LORD and made vows to him."

Think about that. Jonah tried to rebel and go his own way. God not only guided him to where He wanted him to go in the first place, but He used the excursion as an opportunity to convert new followers.

The point is, God uses our *whole* journey and the story that goes with it. There are lots of people who go to school and get good grades, then graduate, get a job, and climb the corporate ladder. And I'm sure God uses people like that. In fact, I know He does.

But I've come to appreciate how God has shown up in the details of my story and in my life. I was embarrassed when I finished last in my high school class. Now I thank God for the opportunity to share that detail to show how unbelievable it is that I would go on to own a group of business schools.

It was really tough for me when my back started to give out after my time working in the factory for Cannon Mills. It's never easy when your body fails you.

I was confused when I was told that I had no aptitude for sales and that I would never be a successful salesperson. That hurt my pride. But now I celebrate that obstacle as another testament to what God can do when you bring Him into your life.

Ultimately, that path, with the obstacles I had to face, is the one God led me down. Being rejected by the insurance company led me to the business school. My time at the Evans Business School, first as a student, and then as an owner, would lead me everywhere else I was meant to go.

Like Jonah, I ended up where I was supposed to be. While I may not have left behind a ship full of men who saw what God did in real time and began to worship Him, hopefully, as I have the opportunity to share my stories with others, the people who hear them see a God-sized ripple in the places I've been.

The Evans Business School certainly was one of those places—not that I knew it when taking classes there. At the time, I didn't even know if I could afford to go there.

During my meeting with the director, I found out that the school operated on the quarters system, and the next quarter would start in a few weeks. I also learned that, although it was more than I could afford as a broke young man, the tuition was quite reasonable. The school had a work-study program for some of its students.

I took classes in business administration and accounting. I realized that, unlike the stuff I had studied in high school, I not only was interested in this material but seemed to have a knack for it. Something just clicked for me in understanding how being good at business would lead me to a more comfortable future. I had seen my dad, who was very good at business, become successful. He owned the service station but also branched out into other more entrepreneurial ventures. I think if he hadn't died so young, he would have been even more successful.

I'd also seen my mom, who didn't have the background or knowledge in these areas, struggle to keep things running and profitable. Ultimately, I think that lack of expertise cost us our home and businesses and shaped a lot of my youth.

Being in those classrooms in the Evans Business School, I realized I had a chance to change my life. But first I needed to stay in school.

Between tuition, meals, and gas for my car, I needed more money, so I went back on the hunt for another job. I checked the classified ads and went to different businesses I thought might be hiring that could be a good fit for me. Every place I walked into, I was told no. Finally, I filled out an application at a bakery in Kannapolis. The manager said they weren't hiring at the moment but told me he would let me know if he had something for me.

Curious about what working for a bakery would be like, I walked around the back to check out the equipment. I noticed among the employees someone I had gone to school with. Taking it as a good sign, I started asking him about his hours, what he did, and how much he got paid. It all sounded great to me.

That was on a Friday. After spending all weekend thinking about it, I showed up at 5:00 a.m. the following Monday and started working. There was only one problem: I hadn't actually been hired. I figured the best way to get hired was by making a good impression. So, every morning I went down to the bakery where the trucks would be loaded for that day's deliveries. I did anything I was asked to do, kept a good attitude, and hustled to complete each task to the best of my ability, just as if they were paying me to do it. When Friday came around, the manager went to each employee handing out envelopes. When he got to me, he realized he didn't have anything with my name on it.

"You're doing a great job, son. Who are you?"

"My name is George Shinn, sir," I replied.

"Have you been working this week?"

"I've been here working all week," I said.

The manager frowned. "No . . . I mean, have you been *employed* here?"

It reminded me of the insurance salesman, and I was suddenly worried. Had I failed this test too?

"Well, no sir," I said shyly.

"You mean you've been working here all week without being hired?"

"Yes, sir."

"Son, you were the best employee we had this week. Let's make sure to get you paid."

I was so relieved.

Working at the bakery was rewarding, and the paycheck that came with it was useful as well. The lesson I learned through this experience, though, was even more valuable than the check: show up and work hard, and good things will happen.

However, there was a problem: what the bakery paid me wasn't enough to cover my bills at school.

Frustrated and embarrassed, I told the school director that I couldn't afford the tuition.

"I'm sorry," I said. "I like being here. But I don't have the money."

The director, Howard Graham, told me that he would help me get a part-time job so I could afford to keep attending the school.

"Mr. Graham," I told him, "I'm having a hard enough time keeping up with the classes as it is. If I get another part-time job, there's no way I can make the grades to stay in school. These kinds of classes aren't for slow folks like me."

"Okay, then," Mr. Graham said. "Let me make another suggestion. I've got a part-time job for you here. That shouldn't bother you one bit, because it's right here at the school. I need you to stay here and sweep up, dust all the erasers, wash the chalkboards, and fill up all the vending machines we have here for food five days a week, Monday through Friday. It shouldn't take you more than a couple of hours a day. If you do that, I'll cover your tuition."

I said yes, and we shook hands.

Unfortunately, a new term was starting, which meant I had to buy more books. I didn't have money for that either. Once again, I went to the director and told him I was broke.

"I thought you might be coming back to see me," Mr. Graham said. "I tell you what. If you're willing to clean the bathrooms, including the toilets, and mop the floors on the weekend, I'll cover your books too."

"Sounds good to me," I told Mr. Graham. "But one question: Does this mean I'm the janitor?" I asked.

"I guess technically it does," he said. "But your title will be *custodian*."

I liked the idea of being a custodian a lot better than being a janitor.

This made for long days at school, but I've never been afraid of working long days. Plus, I had started seeing a girl socially who I'd met in class. Her name was Carolyn Smith, and she was smart, funny, very easy to look at, and we always had a good time when we would see each other outside of school.

One Saturday morning, I'd been at the school cleaning the toilets and tidying up. Carolyn and I were scheduled to go on a date later that day.

The only problem was, I was living back in Kannapolis, and she lived in Concord. It didn't make much sense—nor could I afford—to drive forty-five minutes after my shift to shower and change, only to turn around and drive back to pick her up. The school didn't have a shower, but I made do with the sink and towels. It wasn't the most deluxe accommodations, but it was better than the alternative. Carolyn never seemed to mind.

I was just about to head out after finishing my grooming activities when I heard a knock at the door. No one else was in the building, and the door was locked. For someone to be knocking on a Saturday was sort of unusual since the school was closed. Imagine my surprise when I looked out the window only to find two attractive young girls at the door.

Needless to say, I opened the door immediately.

"Hello!" one of the girls said cheerily. "Do you work here?"

I paused, only briefly. "Why, yes. Yes, I do."

"Wonderful!" the girl exclaimed, a twinkle of energy in her eyes. "We're thinking about enrolling in classes, so we would love to see the school. Can you show us around?"

"Well . . . I don't see why not," I said. Technically, I did work there. As a part-time custodian and student, I was very well acquainted with the campus.

I led the two girls on a tour of the business school. More than the physical spaces the classrooms were in, I talked about the opportunities those classrooms represented to the students enrolled there. I knew that very well. In my time as a student, I could already tell my future was changing. Even though I was only a part-time custodian and relatively new business school student, I still knew enough to conclude the tour by handing the girls applications for the school and catalogs that detailed the class offerings for the next quarter.

Then I locked up and headed out for my date with Carolyn.

The following Monday, I was in class when those two girls (plus three of their friends) came by the front office with completed applications in hand. The office staff were of course pleased to see new students who were ready to enroll, but there was one small problem: the girls kept asking for Mr. Shinn and said they would only turn in their applications to him.

No one in the office knew of a Mr. Shinn who worked as a recruiter.

"Maybe I'm confused," the administrator said, and she asked the girls to please wait there.

She went and spoke with Mr. Graham, the head of the school. "That's got to be George," he said. "He was the only one here that day. He's in accounting class now."

Imagine my surprise when I was called out of class to come to the office.

"Did I do something wrong?" I asked the person who came into my classroom to get me.

"No, it's nothing like that," they replied.

Any hesitation or concern I had quickly disappeared when I walked into the office and saw the two girls, applications in hand.

"Mr. Shinn! We are here and ready to enroll!" one of the girls said excitedly as she ran up and gave me a hug.

The only logical thing to do was to sign them up for the courses. Just like when I cleaned the toilets, I saw enrolling new students as just another example of being willing to do any job that needed doing.

It was an incredibly impactful evening in my life and in the lives of others.

Carolyn, the girl I was washing up to go see, would eventually become my wife.

The girls who came by the college that night (and their friends) would enroll for the new quarter—and I got a promotion that day. The director was impressed with the whole episode and asked if I would be interested in sitting down with the owner of the school. I didn't see why not.

That meeting would change my life.

I hit it off with the owner, Mr. Ratchford, and could sense I was walking down a path toward something bigger than I could have expected. He offered me a job as a student recruiter, earning ten dollars for every new student I enrolled while continuing my education at the school and still having my tuition and books covered.

I wasn't going to get rich at ten dollars per head. Still, it was a chance to make more money than I had made in any other job.

I did what my mom told me to do: I worked hard and trusted God with the rest. And wouldn't you know it, God showed up in a major way.

There were four other recruiters: two retired schoolteachers in their sixties and two full-time trained salespeople. By the time the next term started, I had recruited and enrolled more students than all four of them combined.

The owner was so impressed that he offered me a full-time job as a recruiter for all of his schools, in addition to the one I had been recruiting for, as soon as I graduated. Now I was the one going to high schools, giving speeches and presentations about the kind of opportunities a business school meant.

I couldn't believe it. Me? Going back to high schools voluntarily? The kid who had stuttered giving public presentations? Because I was so young, I was able to talk to the current students—many of whom I was friends with—to get leads as recruits for other possible students. It was my first lesson in how to use your existing customers to grow your future business.

I was able to grow the business quite well.

Going into schools and convincing students to enroll in business school, while making good money, all without a college degree, was pretty exciting for me.

It sure beat the cotton mills.

The school in Concord showed real improvement after my first year. The other schools, however—despite increased attendance—were still in financial trouble.

I suggested to the owner that, since he lived in Concord, he keep that school and sell the other three. He said he didn't think he'd be able to find anyone to buy them, but maybe he could find someone to take them over.

"Well, I could do that," I offered. He took me up on it and let me assume ownership and control of schools in Greensboro, Raleigh, and Durham. It didn't cost me any money, and Mr. Ratchford wouldn't be losing money anymore.

So, there I was, in charge of my own schools in Greensboro, Raleigh, and Durham and taking advantage of a chance to work my tail off to see what I could do.

I was so grateful that the path I had taken in life, or the path God had led me down, had shaped me for this opportunity. I hadn't been a good student in high school and didn't have the opportunity to go to a traditional four-year university. Now it was my job to identify, connect with, and convince others like me to consider a business college.

Part of the reason I hadn't been a good student earlier in my life was because I had a stutter, which contributed to a lack of self-confidence. Thanks to my old teacher Mrs. Drummond, and the hours of attention she gave me, I not only spoke without stuttering but could get up in front of a group of people and share the incredible opportunities our colleges had to offer.

I think about that sometimes. When Jonah was in the belly of the fish, he probably wasn't thinking, *Things are going exactly how they're supposed to, so I don't have anything to worry about here.*

In fact, Jonah 2:2 tells us that Jonah cried out to God from deep inside this fish in the middle of the sea. "In my distress I called to the LORD, and he answered me. From deep in the realm of the dead I called for help, and you listened to my cry."

Psalm 34:4 says, "I sought the LORD, and he answered me; he delivered me from all of my fears." Note that it doesn't say "some of my fears" or "many of my fears." It says *all of them.*

I was realizing how God was using the hard parts of my life to shape me for His purposes.

God's greatest desire for our lives is to be in community with Him. He often uses our struggles and despair, those moments in our lives when we have no other option but to lean on Him, to bring us into that most intimate sense of a God-sized embrace. But He also uses the strange and unusual paths we take as an outline of the way He shapes our lives.

How in the world did Jonah get onto dry land by way of a fish? Only because of God. How did I end up with the opportunity—as someone who was on free lunch, finished last in their class, and was cleaning toilets and bathing in the college bathroom—of being a part owner in that company?

It was because of God. It still is.

I felt like I was heading down a divine path. I was a young man who was now entering a world of possibility I never dreamed of. I could hear my mother's words in my ear. "If you're gonna partner with God, you better dream big."

I had the "dream big" part down. I would soon come to learn a lot more about what it meant to partner with God.

CHAPTER 6

You Can't Outwork Your Need for God

One of my favorite aspects of the story of Joseph is the lessons it has for those who aspire to or end up in leadership. There's no question that Joseph, as the second in command to Pharaoh, was a great leader. With God's help, he saw the threat of famine coming for the people of Israel and Egypt and made a plan that guided their people through it.

But before Joseph was elevated to a position of authority, he had to be obedient in a position of obscurity. He was not in a position of high authority when Potiphar's wife tried to seduce him. He was a servant in someone else's home. He had been abandoned by his family and sold into slavery. He didn't know if he would ever return home, let alone see his father again.

You could understand if Joseph, at that moment with Potiphar's wife, thought, *Well, what has God done for me lately?* and given in to temptation.

But he didn't.

Joseph was obedient. The Bible records the answer Joseph gave Potiphar's wife:

With me in charge . . . my master does not concern
himself with anything in the house; everything he
owns he has entrusted to my care. No one is greater in
this house than I am. My master has withheld nothing
from me except you, because you are his wife. How
then could I do such a wicked thing and sin against
God? (Genesis 39:8–9)

Joseph was obedient to God in a moment when he was
unsupervised by any other man. No one would have known if
he had given in to temptation—except God.

But who matters more than God?

Joseph's loyalty and obedience to God in a position of
obscurity led directly to his later elevation to a position
of authority. Looking back, I can see a similar pattern in
my own life and career. Before God would elevate me to
different positions of authority, whether it was owning
the Hornets basketball team or devoting more time and
resources to ministry after I sold it, I had to walk through
my own trials and temptations.

That journey taught me to be obedient and to bring God
into all aspects of my life—especially my business life. It wasn't
easy at first.

I owned five business schools at thirty years old. The schools
I took over from Dave Ratchford (who was the Concord Clerk
of Court) were the ones that were struggling the most.

Mr. Ratchford had been a great boss. But he was, first
and foremost, a businessman. He didn't let me take over
the top-earning schools. The schools I owned in Durham,
Fayetteville, Greensboro, and Raleigh were the lowest earners.
Given my track record as a recruiter, and with the skills I'd

learned as a student in the business schools, I thought I could turn them around.

Our schools were regularly in financial trouble, and that led to some hard conversations. Being in that spot was a great training ground for me. On one occasion, I was $20,000 short and couldn't come up with that kind of money. I was faced with an incredibly difficult moment: either close the school or not pay my staff.

I'll never forget having to look the teachers and staff of my school in the eye and tell them that we couldn't pay them. I felt like my mom, who, despite her best efforts to keep our businesses running after my dad died, ultimately had to watch her home go up for sale at the auction.

Just like He'd done back then, God provided through the people He had put in my life.

I told the staff we were $20,000 short and that closing the school was an option. The mood was somber, but the employees were incredibly understanding.

A few years earlier, when I had just started in my role as an owner, Mr. Ratchford and I had examined the financials for King's College in Raleigh, and we realized we needed to make some adjustments, specifically to how much we were spending on salaries. We ultimately decided I needed to fire Britt, the highest-paid person on the payroll.

I drove up to Raleigh the next day and met with Jimmy Carter, the president of the college at the time (and not the person who would later become president of the country).

"Jimmy," I began, "we need to fire Britt Dorman. We have to cut salaries, and his is the highest."

"You can't fire Britt," Jimmy protested. "He doesn't just teach; he opens the building in the morning, teaches all day, collects the tuition, makes the schedules, comes back to teach night classes, and then locks the building when he's done. He practically does everything."

I had to admit, Jimmy was making a compelling case. But I still needed to cut the salaries somehow.

"Okay, Jimmy," I said. "You're right. I won't fire Britt. I'm going to fire you."

Jimmy was stunned, but I was serious. I fired him on the spot and put Britt in charge that day. The school's performance improved some under Britt's leadership, but we were still in a hole—a $20,000 hole.

After the staff meeting where I informed them of the shortfall, Britt came up to me privately.

"George," Britt said softly, "I have exactly $20,000 in my life savings. It's all the money I have in the world. I've been saving it for a rainy day. But . . . "

He paused and looked me in the eye.

I could feel myself starting to cry while Britt continued.

"I've never believed in anybody more than I do you. I trust you with everything I've got. Take my money and use it to keep the school going, then pay me back when you can."

Britt wrote me a check for $20,000. I took it, paid off the debt, and kept the school open.

In the Gospel of Mark, we read what Jesus told His disciples about giving. After watching a crowd of people make donations to the temple treasury, with many wealthy people donating "large amounts," Jesus saw a poor widow come and put in just two coins.

"Truly I tell you," Jesus told His disciples, "this poor widow has put more into the treasury than all the others. They all gave out of their wealth; but she, out of her poverty, put in everything—all she had to live on" (Mark 12:43–44).

Britt's faithfulness and generosity and the other employees' offer to teach without pay ranked as the greatest, truest example of that sentiment I've ever seen. I knew exactly what those teachers were making. I knew that Britt, despite having that much money in savings, wasn't wealthy. Their demonstrations and offers of support were the real-life manifestations of God's love for me. I can see that now. I also see how, throughout my life, God has always surrounded me with love and reminders of His presence, just waiting for me to realize it and love Him back.

I'm thankful He has been so patient with me. Because, even after that, I still thought I could make things happen on my own.

I'd like to say that, on the heels of Britt's generosity, I turned everything around and became an overwhelmingly successful businessman . . . but that wouldn't be right. Britt had given me some money, but he hadn't changed my heart—not the way it needed to be changed.

As a result, our business continued to struggle.

It seemed like the same pattern. Part of the appeal of our schools was our affordable tuition, so raising prices to increase revenue wasn't necessarily a workable solution. Our product was good. Our students learned and were improving their lives with the education they were receiving. We taught people how to act, look, and dress professionally and how to do everything—and I mean *everything*—with enthusiasm.

But I had to enthusiastically scramble around constantly to keep the schools afloat. I was able to cover the payroll and supplies, but taxes were a problem—eventually one that seemed too tough to overcome. By the time I was thirty, my schools had accrued a substantial tax bill. I began looking for someone to work with me on a payment plan. The government is decidedly less than understanding and flexible.

I went to every bank I could find in North Carolina. They may have had different names, logos, and slogans, but they all had one thing in common: they all told me no.

Running out of options, I decided to turn to some experts. I scheduled a meeting with two CPAs and an attorney to review my situation and come up with some options. The session cost $500, which was a lot of money. Even though I was in debt, I figured it was the only way to get me out of my predicament.

I brought all my financial records to this meeting and laid everything out for the professionals. I had a decent amount of students coming in each term, and they had to pay their tuition for the quarter in advance. I thought if I could just buy enough time to make it to the start of the next quarter, maybe I could be okay. I was hoping that the accountants would agree with me and that the lawyer would help me figure out a way to make it happen.

That's not what they did.

The professionals huddled with me for a while and asked lots of questions about specific projections and revenue streams. Then they wanted to discuss it among themselves and asked me to wait outside.

After what seemed like an eternity, they called me back into the room. Instead of offering me a plan of attack, they told me to surrender.

"George, we have gone over everything thoroughly," the lawyer said somberly. "I'm afraid there is nothing we can do for you. Our best advice is that you file for bankruptcy."

I was shocked, disappointed, and even a little angry.

"Bankruptcy?!" I stammered. "What do you mean? I'm not filing bankruptcy. I can't even afford to file bankruptcy. Didn't you look at my earning projections? I'm gonna make enough money."

One of the accountants shook his head dismissively.

"Your earnings projections are a pipe dream. That's what you *hope* you will do. That's not a viable economic indicator, and you can't borrow money on it."

After a few more questions from me and rejections from them, I gathered my things and headed to the elevator.

The attorney, who was the senior member of the team, walked me out. As we waited for the elevator, he offered what he thought was a comforting thought.

"George, you have a lot of potential. But this business isn't for you. Why don't you let these schools go and get a job working for somebody else?"

The elevator door opened, and I started to step inside. Honestly, this was a conversation I was glad to be leaving.

Before I could get in the elevator, though, the man grabbed my shoulder and looked me in the eyes.

"You don't have a prayer, George. Not a prayer."

The man had clearly never worked as a motivational speaker.

The elevator door closed, and I was left alone with his parting, hurtful words.

Not a prayer? I thought. It felt like I was back in that insurance office, being told I would never work in sales.

Was it really that bad? Did I really have no hope at all?

I didn't want to accept that, and I really didn't want to declare bankruptcy, so I spent the next several days continuing my hunt for funding from any bank I could think of.

A few days after that meeting, I was driving back from Raleigh on Interstate 85, having been rejected by even more banks.

I was embarrassing myself with these bankers, practically begging them to loan me enough money to make it until the next batch of high school graduates would enroll.

None of them said yes.

I was at the end of the line. My employees were once again working without a paycheck, but even as supportive as they'd been, they needed to be paid. My tax bill was still out there, and I had no money. I had stopped sleeping at night because I was so overwhelmed by the stress and concerns. I had no idea what to do.

The parting words of the attorney continued to haunt me. *I don't have a prayer*, I kept thinking. *I don't have a prayer.*

As I drove, I could suddenly hear my mother's advice. It was the same advice she'd given me when I was a young boy and at every stage of my life since: "The two keys to success in life, Junior, are to pray a lot and work your tail off."

I knew I had the hard work part down . . . but I was definitely leaving out the prayers.

In fact, I'd been so consumed with my problems, I'd honestly forgotten about God in some significant ways. I'd been working so much that I had stopped going to church and reading the Bible. Honestly, I had stopped praying too.

Looking back on it now, it's easy to see how my focus on problems led me to forget about the solution. God is always the answer, regardless of the question.

Right then, as I was driving down I-85, I started praying.

"Lord," I said, "I clearly need Your help. I tried doing this on my own, and I forgot about You. You know how big of a mess I'm in. I'm so sorry. Please help me."

It felt strange to just talk to God out loud like that, but as I continued driving and the words kept coming, I could feel my mind, and heart, changing.

Suddenly, I heard myself saying things I'd never thought, let alone said, before.

"Please become my partner, Lord. Be my Chairman of the Board. You do the guiding, and I will do whatever work You tell me to do. Whatever happens, I will share everything I have with You, and I will tell the world what You've done for me.

"Please, Lord," I continued. "Help me."

As the words continued to pour out, I could feel my body physically reacting.

I don't know if the *car* was shaking or if *I* was shaking as tears poured down my face. All I know was that I couldn't see the road through all my tears. I had to pull over on the side of the interstate. My eyes weren't just leaking; I was full-on sobbing.

The lawyer told me I didn't have a prayer, and I had been begging the banks for help. Now I was begging again, only this time it felt right.

I was crying so much that I had to use my jacket sleeves to wipe my eyes. The shining sun seem magnified through my tears, like I was staring right into it. I will never forget sitting there on the side of the road, feeling literally overwhelmed and blinded in the presence of God.

I don't know how long I stayed there weeping and praying. Eventually, the tears stopped, and I pulled back onto I-85. Everything was the same as it was before I pulled over, but somehow, everything was different too. None of my worldly circumstances had changed. I was still in a mountain of debt. I was still broke. I still had no idea how I was going to pay my employees or keep my business open.

But in the car that afternoon, I realized I wasn't the one in charge anymore. I had a new Chairman of the Board—and God was big enough for all those problems and a whole lot more.

Jesus told His followers many times not to worry. In His Sermon on the Mount, Jesus reminds us that the birds of the air "neither sow nor reap nor gather into barns," but God still cares for and feeds them. And He asked the crowd, "Are you not of more value than they? And which of you by being anxious can add a single hour to his span of life?" (Matthew 6:26–27 ESV).

Jesus promises us that, if we follow and learn from Him, He will give us rest. "My yoke is easy and my burden is light," He said (Matthew 11:28–30).

That day, maybe for the first time in my life, I understood what He meant.

Not all of us are like Joseph, who never lost his faith—even when held in slavery or faced with temptation. Some of us come around much later in life.

Life with Jesus was suddenly easier.

My problems were still there.

But so was God.

CHAPTER 7
My New Chairman of the Board

The book of Acts tells us how Saul, a Pharisee and murderous persecutor of Christians, was traveling to Damascus when Jesus appeared to him. Jesus revealed Himself as the promised Messiah and called Saul to radically change his life.

The experience literally left this terrified religious official blind and helpless. After Saul spent three days praying and fasting, God restored Saul's vision and called him into service. Saul declared Jesus to be the risen Son of God, was baptized, and was given a new name: Paul—the apostle who took the message of Christ to Gentiles (non-Jews) and wrote much of the New Testament. He spent the rest of his life traveling and preaching the gospel of Jesus Christ. His life was totally different after he met Jesus.

That's how powerful God is. He turned His fiercest opponent into one of the Christian faith's greatest champions. Now, I never persecuted Christians, but it's fair to say there were times when I didn't look much like someone who followed Jesus. But after my own roadside conversion on I-85, God showed up in my life in some new and amazing ways.

I drove straight back to my office once I got back on the interstate that day. And wouldn't you know it? God gave me a chance to trust Him right away.

Back then, publishing companies delivered our textbooks and then billed us for them afterward. Because of my previous problems with payment, however, we'd recently been informed that they would only ship them to us COD, or Cash on Delivery.

That was a problem for me because I couldn't pay for the books until a new semester started and the students had paid their tuition. It was a difficult situation I had been avoiding. I'd previously told my assistant not to put any of their calls through to me, no matter what. She was told to make up any excuse necessary to keep me away from them until I could figure this out.

Basically, I told her to lie.

So who do you think called me almost as soon as I got back to the office?

I don't think I even had time to hang up my jacket when my assistant buzzed in, telling me that the man from the publisher was on the phone. To her surprise, I calmly told her I would take the call.

Having God at the wheel somehow held back my fear and worry about what the man on the phone would say or how things would work out.

The man asked if he could send all the books for the new quarter, and I calmly explained that I didn't have enough money to pay him when they showed up. But I also told him I would, eventually, be able to pay him in full. The reality was, if he didn't, I really wouldn't have a prayer. I needed the books to enroll new students.

"Well, you're a good customer," the man told me. "Can you send me *some* money at least?"

"I can absolutely do that," I told him. "You send me the books, I'll send you what I can afford now, and I will pay you the rest when the students enroll."

After I hung up the phone, I called my assistant and asked her to come in with the checkbook to see what we had in the account. As I suspected, it wasn't much.

"Please send the publisher one dollar."

My assistant looked at me like I was speaking a foreign language.

First I had taken the call, and now I was having her do this.

"It'll be okay," I explained. "God is in charge. If any other creditors call, I'll be happy to talk to them too."

Several days later, I got another call from the publisher. He didn't sound happy.

"Mr. Shinn," he started. "I got your check. I think there must be some mistake."

I took a deep breath and just prayed, *Lord, this is me trusting You.*

"You sent me a one dollar bill," the publisher informed me.

"Yes sir, that's right," I confirmed. For a few seconds, the publisher didn't say anything. Finally, he replied, "Are you trying to be cute?"

"No sir," I said seriously. "I understand why you're asking. But I am being sincere. I told you I would pay you what I could afford. The reality is, one dollar was all I could afford. But, because you were patient and got us the books we needed for the start of the new quarter, I now have more tuition money I can send you. You will be paid in full."

Even though I wasn't sure how the publisher would react, I was overwhelmed with a sense of calm. I'd spent so much time dancing and dodging and flirting with the edge of deception, and none of it had worked.

Now I could feel God giving me the confidence to just be honest.

It worked with the books, so I started telling a lot of other people how much money I *didn't* have for them.

The following week, I called a meeting with the ten key people in our company. These people were not only loyal employees but good friends. With one exception, I wasn't sure how many of them, if any, had a relationship with God. After the usual round of casual chitchat at the start, everyone eventually stopped talking and turned their eyes toward me. I was the one who had called the meeting, and they were all wondering why they were there.

Oddly, I was more nervous in this meeting than I had been on the phone with the publisher. Once again, I asked God for a sense of calm and then said, "Before we begin, I want to start this meeting with a prayer." Everyone exchanged surprised glances. "Please bow your heads."

I offered a quick prayer, and when I had finished, I heard several employees say, "Amen."

Recognizing that we had never begun a meeting in prayer before, I wanted to explain to my team who our new Chairman of the Board was.

"I want to tell you a story about what happened to me on I-85 the other day," I began.

I tried to stay unemotional about the experience when telling the story, but I kept getting choked up. In fact, I still get choked up to this day when I think about it or when I share what happened. Something about sensing God's divine presence and the comfort and care I felt makes me feel so vulnerable that the tears just come.

After I finished the story, I got to the main point.

"I want you all to know that you don't work for George Shinn anymore. As of now, we are all working for the Lord."

In some ways, this was a much harder test of trusting the Lord than the phone call with the publisher had been. I already had the books at that point; the publisher was just waiting on the money. All our decisions had already been made, and we were both waiting for the results to materialize.

But these employees did have to make a choice, a choice they made each and every day to get up, leave their homes, and come to work for me. They had to believe and trust that I would eventually be able to pay them. So, for them to hear me say I was now working for God, and so were they, had to be fairly unexpected. They seemed a little taken aback, but I knew in time, and with a consistent deference to God in the workplace, I could show them that my faith, and dedication to involving God in our professional lives, was sincere.

But God shows up in the most unexpected places all the time. That's how you know it's God. It's trusting Him to keep doing it that can prove challenging.

I love the story of Elijah in the Old Testament. Elijah was a prophet whose job was to talk to the king of Israel and deliver God's message to the people.

The king at the time, Ahab, had taken a wife named Jezebel, who worshipped a different god. Elijah knew that Ahab and Jezebel's worship of a false god would be catastrophic for the people of Israel. The prophet warned the king there would be a severe drought as a result of Ahab and Jezebel's disobedience to the one true God.

As you might expect, Ahab didn't appreciate Elijah's message, and the king threatened the prophet's life. God told Elijah to flee to the desert and await further instructions. Soon after, the Lord promised to provide for Elijah, who would be fed by ravens.

Just think about Elijah's instructions from God in that moment. First, speak uncomfortable truths to the most important person in the land, then go hide in the desert and wait around for Me and trust that birds will bring you food.

Elijah was obedient, and God responded by doing many amazing things in Elijah's life and the lives of those around him—not the least of which was having ravens bring him food in the desert.

With God now in charge of my company, I had to rely on Him to provide. That meant trusting Him to guide my steps and listening closely for His voice, even when what He said didn't seem to make much sense.

I think a lot of people struggle with envisioning what trusting God looks like in their everyday lives. What does it truly mean to invite Him into every space, personally, professionally, and spiritually? For me, it looked like a few different things.

For starters, the first thing I did when I woke up every day was talk to God.

"Good morning, Lord!" I would say as I looked out the window. Before my roadside revelation, I had a hard time sleeping, so waking up wasn't something I was excited about. I saw each new day as one that would bring more challenges and probably frustrations. Now I saw it as a new day to be in God's presence. I really did feel Him next to me. Greeting Him in the morning really was like talking to someone in the room with me.

Sensing God by my side, it was easy to acknowledge Him throughout the day. At work, I started every meeting with a quick prayer. After some initial surprise, my employees began to realize this was going to be how things were from now on. Years later, I heard from people who worked for me that it was the first time they'd ever seen anyone pray at work. Seeing someone casually but intentionally involve God in their work life had an impact on their own faith.

Here's the crazy part: The more I involved God, the easier things got in my life. Whether it was conversations with employees, vendors, students, or their parents, I was at ease and calm when I brought God into the conversation. I'm not saying everything worked out in my favor, but I did have the sense that I could turn over my problems—any problem— to the Lord, and that made it no longer my problem. In the process of turning over my problems to God, I felt Him caring for me. When it came time for me to handle those problems, it seemed like they always worked out, somehow, some way.

In fact, I came to realize that these problems were actually opportunities God presented to me so I could learn and become stronger. Rather than bemoaning these obstacles, I accepted God's challenge head-on, knowing His guidance would get me through.

One day I got word that the founder of one of the top business schools in the country, Jack Jones, was coming to North Carolina, looking at possible opportunities for expansion or acquisition.

Jack ran the nonprofit Jones College, based in Jacksonville, and also operated a large network of private schools throughout

Florida. Even the possibility that he was in North Carolina looking to grow his business's footprint made him a direct competitor to me.

But rather than become defensive or fearful about the impact Jack might have on my life and business, I felt the Lord urging me to lean in. "Maybe there is something he can teach you," I felt God saying. "Maybe you can learn from him."

I followed God's prompting and reached out to see if Jack would be willing to meet with me. I also offered him my help. I knew the landscape in North Carolina better than he did, and I told him I would help him any way I could.

I scheduled a meeting with him in Jacksonville. I caught a flight the day of the appointment and went straight to his office at the Jones College headquarters, where I was told that Jack was out of the office. In fact, he was out of town.

His assistant was incredibly apologetic, but I was nice, understanding, and even offered the idea that it might have been my mistake. His assistant assured me it wasn't.

I flew back to North Carolina. By the time I had returned, I had a message from Jack, apologizing for his mistake.

"I will make it up to you," Jack told me. And he did.

Jack and I started talking about how his business had become so successful.

"What do you do for the veterans here in North Carolina?" he asked me.

"Veterans?" I responded. "Not too much. What should we be doing?"

It turns out, we should have been doing quite a bit.

Because many veterans had never enrolled in college, they were leaving the military without the education and skills they needed to succeed in the workforce. The government offered fantastic education benefits, covering the cost of tuition for business schools as well as traditional colleges and universities.

Jack's colleges had been identifying, recruiting, and working with veterans for some time. This wasn't just a useful clientele; it was integral to their business model. Jack made it incredibly clear that reaching out to veterans should be a top priority for us.

That meeting was a turning point for our company and for me.

I immediately focused on recruiting veterans and explaining the benefits they would gain attending our schools. Our profit margins began to increase dramatically, and I learned a valuable lesson on the importance of trusting God.

Before my meeting with Jack Jones, I didn't know recruiting veterans was something we should be doing. Without God telling me to reach out to Jack, I don't think I would have ever thought of asking a direct competitor for advice. In fact, I'm sure I wouldn't have thought of that.

God opened doors for me I hadn't known existed. All I had to do was trust in Him enough to be willing to walk through them, even if I didn't understand the reasons at the time.

This further cemented in my mind how important it was having God as my Chairman of the Board.

With God in charge, I knew we could be successful. And because God was in charge, I knew I needed to use whatever opportunities He put in my life to help build His kingdom. As I've tried hard to do that over the years, I think God has protected me, despite my many failings.

I have learned that faith means understanding that God knows things we don't know. He hears things we don't hear. He sees things we don't see. Faith tells me that if He's chosen me,

He's going to work around those obstacles to help me accomplish my goal.

After that, I saw my story as God's story. Just like God used that big fish to send Jonah to where He wanted him to go, I saw God guiding my steps as I looked back on my life. I saw His hand in putting me with a single mother, where I learned to appreciate anything and everything I had. I learned to be strong and willing to do dirty jobs like clean toilets and mop floors to accomplish my goals. And then I saw God sending those two girls to the door of that college one Saturday afternoon, which was a fish of its own kind. Those girls are what got me out of the toilet business and into the people business. But I didn't do that—God did.

I had finished last in my high school class, but here I was meeting with one of the most successful owners of business colleges in the country. I was not only learning from Jack Jones but would be able to help him as well.

Whenever something in life doesn't make much sense, it might just be an indication that God is behind it. Just ask Paul. He experienced that on the road to Damascus.

God was behind my meeting with Jack Jones. And He would be behind the incredible things that happened to my business—and to me—as a result.

CHAPTER 8

God-Sized Growth

The Bible is filled with stories that remind us about the virtues of generosity. Not only is it the way God commanded us to live, but Jesus reminds us often of how God rewards a generous heart with abundant provision.

The Bible tells us the story of Jesus feeding five thousand people with five loaves of bread and two fish (Matthew 14:13–21). But the story we learn as children in Sunday school is rich with application for our adult lives and demonstrates a truth I've seen play out in my own.

The story, which is included in all four gospels, comes to us first in the book of Matthew, where we read that Jesus and His disciples were followed by a large crowd. When Jesus saw them, He had compassion on them and healed the sick members of that group.

Then, as dinnertime neared, Jesus's disciples came and told Him that, since it was such a remote place, Jesus should "send the crowds away, so they can go to the villages and buy themselves some food" (Matthew 14:15).

I'm sure it seemed perfectly reasonable at the time, but the idea of anyone telling Jesus what to do just makes me laugh.

Instead, Jesus commanded His disciples to feed the crowd. When they protested that they had only five loaves of bread and two fish, Jesus took over. He had everyone sit down, gave thanks for what they had, and then asked His disciples to pass out the food. To everyone's amazement, there was enough to feed all five thousand people with food left over.

That's the story in the book of Matthew, but the version in the Gospel of John adds one interesting and crucial detail. In chapter 6, John records that, after Jesus had a discussion with Philip about how much it would cost to buy food for everyone there, Andrew told Him, "There is a boy here who has five barley loaves and two fish, but what are they for so many?" (John 6:9 ESV).

From there, Jesus blessed the boy's lunch, handed it to the disciples, and fed all five thousand as the loaves and fish multiplied. Sometimes we get caught up in the miracle and forget the fact that the food was there in the first place only because a young boy offered it to Jesus.

I think it's fun to compare the two versions of the same story in the different gospels because of the contrast they offer. On the one hand, you have the disciples, the people who literally and figuratively were the closest to Jesus. When presented with a challenge, they were practical and thought to send the people home so they could feed themselves. On the other hand, you have a small child who was probably there to hear the popular traveling teacher everyone had been talking about. There was no chance of his lunch being sufficient, but this little boy thought—and acted—faithfully. He gave what he had to the Lord and trusted Him to make it be enough.

And, as both versions of the event tell us, Jesus did.

It's the same message Jesus shares when He compares two visions of what it means to be truly generous. He was teaching in the temple one day when a group of wealthy people came by and put gifts into the treasury. He then saw a widow give two small copper coins. Jesus told the crowd, "Truly I tell you, . . . this poor widow has put in more than all the others. All these people gave their gifts out of their wealth; but she out of her poverty put in all she had to live on" (Luke 21:1–4).

As I reflect on how and why God has blessed me the way He has, especially the impact that meeting with Jack Jones had on my life and career, I can't help but be reminded of those biblical examples. Trust me, I didn't set out to honor God by being generous toward Jack. I truly believe it was the Lord acting in and through me. All I did was not get in the way. And for a guy who finished last in his class, it was the smartest thing I could have done.

Jack not only gave me the idea to start recruiting veterans but also told me how to do it. He became a mentor who offered advice and guidance whenever I needed it. The idea about veterans was genius. At that time, we were in the middle of the Vietnam War. The veterans who returned from the war were looking to start a new life. Our business colleges were the perfect way to go about it. Our schedules were flexible, so people could work while taking classes; our enrollment was affordable; and our timeline to graduate was shorter. Veterans were the perfect people for our schools.

If it hadn't been for Jack, I never would have thought about making them part of our community, but they were now at the *center* of our schools—and our revenue began to grow substantially as a result.

Veterans were a game changer for our colleges. Just like the baskets with fish and loaves, more opportunities just kept showing up.

Other colleges, including our competitors, noticed that our schools had started doing so well and asked us for advice. It was almost like God was showing off. "You trusted Me in your lowest moments; now, watch how high we can go."

Jack had shown me how beneficial being openhanded with my time and ideas could be. I didn't hesitate. Even when some of my employees pushed back, saying it was foolish to help our competitors, I reminded them of two things. First, a competitor of ours had helped us, which was the reason we were even in a position to be helpful now. Second, competition was a good thing! The better our competitors were, the more motivated we would be to work harder and become even better. My employees got on board . . . eventually.

Helping competitors forced me to create a new business model and opened up a new line of revenue for me. When the schools that initially reached out to me—most of which were owned by friends of mine—asked what I charged as a consultation fee, I had no idea what to say. Once again, I asked the Lord. God told me to treat everyone fairly. So, I told the schools that if their business didn't improve after our consultation, they wouldn't owe me anything. But if their revenues did increase, they could pay me a percentage.

It might have been risky, but I thought it was the right thing to do. And since I was trusting God, I wasn't worried about the risks.

I started a new company to handle the consulting business, which I called George Shinn and Associates (GSA). We gave very specific guidance to our top recruiters who went into the schools that contracted with us. They simply executed the play-book we had established.

We tried to institute a student-centered focus. Too many salespeople at these schools were focused on money; I focused on relationships. I encouraged the salespeople to get to know their students, invest in helping them in whatever way they could, and get right with God themselves.

"God will bless you," I told the salespeople. "But you've got to let Him into your life."

When it worked—which it usually did—we made 15 percent off every new student these other schools enrolled. The best part was that it was a win-win. My clients were happy because their enrollments were up, and my employees were happy because they were making money on the commissions they were getting. Of course, I was happy to see the revenue of GSA grow, but it was even more gratifying to see my clients succeed. The Lord really is amazing.

God had taken the failing thing I brought to Him in my distress and redeemed it in the most unbelievable way. I had handed Him a broken business on the verge of bankruptcy, and He turned it into two profitable businesses for me *and* improved profits for several other businesses my team worked with. Out of the ashes of my failure, God was producing new growth.

While GSA helped a growing number of schools trying to replicate our success, our own business schools continued to thrive. I rebranded our schools as Rutledge Educational System and leveraged the connections I was making with other schools through GSA consulting to acquire ones under that umbrella. God had turned my business completely around. He was even taking older projects and blessing them in new ways.

As the Vietnam War was winding down, I sensed our veteran business was beginning to decline and that we would need a different way to appeal to prospective students. But rather than thinking of something new and trying to keep up with our changing culture, I returned to some of the core concepts that made me a believer in our business colleges in the first place.

Two programs our colleges offered that I always found incredibly helpful were the Mr. Executive and Nancy Taylor programs. Mr. Executive was touted as "the unique management development program that prepares young men for executive success." It had everything from the right patterns for men's business attire to proper grooming habits. Nancy Taylor was a charm and grooming course for women, but it also consisted of speedwriting and shorthand curriculum. Plus, the curriculum included material on memory training and the power of speech, both of which I had found to be incredibly useful in my own career. I believed in the value of updating the material because of what I had seen it do in my own life.

Of course, much of the material that had originally been published was now, because of changes in the postwar culture, outdated. The curriculum needed to be rewritten, which I saw as an opportunity.

I arranged a meeting with the publisher and told them about my idea. I told them, "If you will reprint these books with updated pictures and new content, I can get all the schools I am affiliated with to buy them for all of their students." At the time, I owned more than thirty schools, and GSA was working with more than a hundred others. I felt like it would be a no-brainer for the publisher.

They didn't see it that way.

They weren't as excited about bringing back and updating the outdated curriculum as I thought they should be. They told me they weren't going to do it.

Are you crazy? I thought. *Am I missing something?*

Even after I presented them with a proposal of the number of books I would buy, they still said no. So I took matters into my own hands.

"Would you be willing to sell me the rights to it?" I asked them.

They eventually told me that if I would buy their existing unsold inventory at retail price, they would include the rights to the curriculum as well. I thought that was a great deal until I found out how many unsold books they still had on hand.

I did what I always did: I countered, offering half of what they were asking.

"That's all I can do."

And all I could do ended up being good enough for them. They sold me their inventory and the rights to the Mr. Executive and Nancy Taylor curriculum.

I went to work on rewriting the books, with Britt Dorman overseeing the project. He really did an incredible job of bringing in new and relevant pictures and examples while keeping the core concepts the same.

I approached McGraw Hill about publishing the new book, but when they said no, I decided to publish the textbook myself. I formed a new company, Key Publishing Company, whose main product was our new textbook that we required for our leadership development and business school curriculum. We positioned it as the essential road map for navigating the modern business landscape.

We designed the cover ourselves, which pictured a smartly dressed, successful businesswoman and two men dressed in suits with white shirts. One of the men was African American, which was unusual for business textbooks at that time.

To promote the book's launch, I took copies to the annual convention of the National Association of Independent Colleges and Universities (NAICU). It was in a typical convention hall with hundreds of schools and vendors squeezed into booths in tightly packed rows. As I got to the main hall, I walked over to see the place the organizers had assigned us. Right next to us, with an army of representatives and fancy banners, was McGraw Hill—the same company that had declined to publish my book. They had free food and cocktails at their booth, and all we had was one little book. But I had a plan.

Ahead of the convention, I had prepared a brochure that showed an empty school desk. I was making the point that empty desks were the biggest problem our industry was facing. I wanted them to understand that our new book would help schools put students in the desks.

I went to the hotel where everyone was staying and introduced myself to the girl at the front desk. I told her I was with NAICU and asked if I could please have the room numbers of everyone who was at the convention so I could remind them about what time things were scheduled to start tomorrow.

It was stretching the truth, but I technically *was* with the association. To my surprise, the young woman handed me a list with the names and room numbers of all the attendees. So, after midnight, I walked to each of the rooms and slipped the brochure under the door so it would be there in the morning when they woke up.

It worked. When the convention started, we had a line a mile long at our booth waiting for our book. The line went right by the entrance to McGraw Hill's booth. It was a massive success. Almost everyone we spoke to said they wanted to buy the book, and we soon gave out all the copies we had brought.

It wasn't just the people at other schools who took notice of our book. McGraw Hill did as well. I got a phone call shortly after the convention from the man who had previously rejected the book idea.

"George," he said apologetically, "man, you proved me wrong. I'd really like to publish your book."

"Well, gee," I replied. (I was going to enjoy this.) "Don't you think it's a little late? I've already published it, and the orders are pouring in."

Last time we talked, all he did was turn me down. This time, he was doing whatever he could to keep me from saying no.

"What if we help you distribute it?"

It didn't take long for me to figure out that would be a great deal.

"Well, what will you pay me?" I asked.

They offered me their normal fee, but I told them that wasn't going to be good enough.

"I've got invitations to speak at just about every state association in the country, and my presentation is my book. I plan on selling a lot of them. So, you're gonna have to do better than that."

They did.

They offered me a much higher percentage of the sales, which I accepted. I kept my word too—the book earned more than $1 million each year for the next five years. That money, combined with the growing revenue streams of the consulting business and the Rutledge Schools themselves, elevated my financial position to a level I couldn't have dreamed of.

From the late 1960s to the early 1970s, God changed my life financially. I made $3,000 one year. The next, I made $30,000. The following year, I made $300,000. Each year, with God as my partner, my income continued to grow tenfold. That's one reason why I say, if you're going to partner with God, you'd better prepare for something big to happen.

God sure did big things through me—not that I was taking any bows or getting too caught up in it. I was so focused on running the businesses and taking care of the things that had to be done day to day that I never stopped to take stock of what exactly was happening. It wasn't until my staff and I were at a party one night and I overheard a financial analyst shooting his mouth off that I even really understood my situation.

"George is making so much money," my financial guy said, "that if he was driving his new car down the road and got a flat tire, he'd be better off just getting another new car than wasting his time changing the tire."

It was a funny line, but it was also humbling. Within four years, God had taken me from a broken, sobbing heap of a man on the side of the road who was facing bankruptcy or worse and had now made me wealthier than I could have imagined.

I tried to be a good steward with the new opportunities God had provided. I was kind to my employees, honest with the clients, and fair with anyone I was dealing with. But I wasn't perfect. I had my vices. In fact, my accountant who was telling the joke had referenced one of them: I still loved cars. And now that I had the means, I wasn't that shy about acquiring them.

When Charles Ricks, a key adviser and one of the best tax experts in the country, suggested that I should look into diversifying my investments by buying into a car dealership, I was intrigued.

"I like it!" I told Charles. "Let's do it. But I'm a Chevrolet guy, and I prefer a Chevrolet dealership."

"Great," he replied. "But you're going to need a partner."

"I don't need a partner," I retorted. "More than that, I don't *want* a partner."

"Well, you might not want one, but you have to have one," he stated. "General Motors requires that, if you're not going to be there full time, then you can't run the dealership. That's why you need the partner."

"That's ridiculous," I complained. "I run thirty business schools now, all of them remotely. I can run this dealership."

"You might be able to," Charles told me finally, "but General Motors won't allow it. Someone has to be there full time, and they have to own 25 percent of the company. That'll be your partner. So, think about who you want it to be."

Selfishly, I didn't like the idea of being required to have a relationship in which someone else could tell me how to run my business. But if I had to have a partner, I knew who it should be.

In all the times I had been to the car dealership in Raleigh to make a purchase, there was one employee who stood out to me. Every time I walked in, Rick impressed me with his attitude, professionalism, and attention to detail. Rather than haggle over prices, Rick went out of his way to make sure I enjoyed the car-buying experience. One time, I had purchased a brand-new Jaguar XKE from him that turned out to be a lemon. After weeks of frustration, I finally called Rick and told him that I was leaving the car on the side of the road, and if he wanted it, he could come pick it up himself.

When I later went to the dealership with the Jaguar's title in hand, I told Rick I was so frustrated that I wanted my money back.

"No problem, George," he said. "If that's what you want, we will do it."

Rick was so calm and smooth in that interaction. I was impressed, especially when I got my money back. And, now without a car to drive, I promptly bought a new Mercedes-Benz roadster from him.

Six months later, when Rick saw me eyeing a car in his showroom while my Mercedes was being serviced, he asked me, "George, if you were going to get that car, what color would you get it in?"

"Probably gold," I told him.

A few weeks later, Rick called me. "George, your car is here."

"What car?" I asked, somewhat taken aback.

"Your gold Mercedes. I figured you'd want it, so I ordered it for you."

I was so impressed by the confidence and attention to detail and customer service, it made me want to do as much business with him as possible.

So, when my accountant told me I needed a business partner for a new car dealership, I knew exactly who to call.

And that's how Rick Hendrick became my business partner.

CHAPTER 9
Taking Pro Sports for a Test Drive

At the age of twenty-six, Rick Hendrick was about to become the youngest Chevrolet dealer in America. Still, I had zero hesitation. He was young, certainly, but I was only in my midthirties myself. At six feet tall, he towered over me, which wasn't all that unusual. We were both from North Carolina—Rick had been born in Warrenton, just south of the Virginia border, but he had grown up on the other side of Lake Gaston, in South Hill, Virginia.

Because he was so young, Rick didn't have the money to buy into the dealership at the 25 percent level. That wasn't a problem for me. I was so sure of Rick's talent and drive to succeed that I was happy to put up the initial amount on his behalf. There was no doubt in my mind that he would be able to pay me back. And, trust me, he has.

We bought into a Chevrolet dealership in Bennettsville, South Carolina, which was about a hundred and ten miles south of Raleigh, where he'd been working. Much like the first business schools I had been permitted to buy into, this dealership in Bennettsville wasn't exactly the crown jewel of the General Motors collection. It didn't even have a showroom for the cars in its inventory. Don't forget this was pre-internet, when the showroom was still the number one way to promote the new cars in your fleet.

Within eighteen months, Rick had the entire dealership turned around. Not only did it now have a showroom but it was actually one of the more profitable dealerships in the area. As the success of that dealership grew, more opportunities came our way. We acquired a City Chevrolet dealership in Charlotte next and applied the same principles and concepts that had made our South Carolina dealership so successful. It helped that Rick and I both liked cars so much; though, true to my word, I was much more hands-off. Rick ran the day-to-day, and he was very good at it.

Within a few years, Rick and I owned dealerships that sold Hondas, Toyotas, BMWs, and Kenworth trucks under a growing consortium of auto dealerships we called Hendrick Automotive Group. It not only had his name, but his literal ownership of the business was expanding. While we had started at a 75/25 split, Rick's stake had grown to 40 percent of the business. Then, one day on the golf course, Rick asked if I would be willing to sell him more stock, enough to make him the majority owner.

He was looking to acquire more dealerships, including some without my investment. At this point, Rick and I weren't just business partners; we were good friends. But even if we hadn't been, I had a genuine desire to see him succeed and was such a believer in his talent and ability that I don't think my approach would have been any different.

"Sure thing, Rick," I told him. "Just tell me what you think a fair price would be and how you want to pay me." Then we shook hands, and that was that.

Rick was a terrific car salesman, but his first love was car racing. He had won numerous competitions for both racing and engineering as a teenager. And now that his auto dealerships were prospering, he had the resources to get back into his first love in a major way.

Rick started a speedboat racing team and, unsurprisingly, found major success. His team won three straight national championships and even set a world record by hitting 222.2 miles per hour. Watching Rick achieve that level of success was truly gratifying for me. I always liked watching things go fast.

However, the faster things go, the more dangerous they become. In 1982, one of Rick's boat drivers, Jimmy Wright, lost control of the boat and slammed into the shore, killing him instantly. That tragedy led Rick to walk away from boat racing.

As Rick would say later, he lost his love of sports that day. It was incredibly painful for him and, by extension, me. Seeing a friend go through that pain and question himself over what he could have done differently to avoid such a tragedy wasn't easy. But Rick's faith helped him take his questions—and his challenges—to God. As tough as it was for me to see a friend go through a season like that, it was also inspirational to see him come out the other side with God's help.

In hindsight, I think that's one way God helped prepare me for my own struggles and seasons of despair. I had a front-row seat watching Rick take hard things to God and seeing the Lord reward Rick for his courage and faith.

Two years later, Rick started a stock car racing team. He went on to have great success and became one of the true icons of the sport.

But Rick's success in professional sports had rekindled something in me as well.

By 1984, Carolyn and I had been married for some time and had been blessed with three wonderful children. It was a fun time in my home, but I was always focused on how I could continue to provide for my family. And now I felt like the Lord was placing a new dream in my heart for how to continue doing that.

Growing up, I'd always been a huge sports fan and had long dreamt of bringing a professional team to Charlotte. Through his success in racing, Rick had made friends with a man named Max Muhleman, a brilliant sports agent with his own marketing firm. Rick asked Max to introduce me to some people who might help make my dream come true.

My first love was baseball, and if I could have snapped my fingers and made something happen, I would have become a baseball owner right away. Max, however, thought the best possibility was professional football.

In the early 1980s, a group of businessmen had started a new football league, called the United States Football League (USFL). Originally conceived of by a New Orleans antiques dealer named David Dixon, the USFL planned on playing football in the spring to avoid direct competition with the NFL. Dixon had grown up when Tulane University football was a national powerhouse, and he remembered seeing big crowds for their spring game. If Tulane—a college team—could draw twenty-five thousand people in the spring, he thought, why couldn't a pro team? Dixon studied the models of football leagues that had and had not worked, and he thought his plan of starting a league that played when people were missing football would be viable.

The league was announced in 1982, and, in 1983, the USFL launched with twelve teams. After that season, a few things happened. The league expanded to eighteen teams and brought in a couple of new owners. New York businessman and real estate mogul Donald Trump purchased the New Jersey Generals, and a businessman from out west named J. William Oldenburg bought the Los Angeles Express.

Donald Trump was famous in New York for his cavalier lifestyle and jet-setting ways, and Oldenburg was the West Coast version of that. Going by the nickname Mr. Dynamite, Oldenburg was an incredibly colorful character who was famous for his Rolls-Royces, private planes, and lavish parties. His company regularly referred to him as a "self-made billionaire." As the new owner of the Express, he lived up to the hype—at least initially.

Oldenburg and the Express announced in April 1984 that they were signing Steve Young, the Brigham Young University quarterback who seemed to be a lock to be the top pick in the upcoming NFL draft. Steve Young's success on the field *and* his contract with the Express set records. Oldenburg signed Young to a forty-million-dollar contract, which would pay out over the next forty-three years. For comparison's sake, Joe Montana, whom Young would eventually replace on the San Francisco 49ers, had a base salary in 1984 of $800,000. Young's contract was insane.

And, as it turns out, unsustainable.

By the end of the 1984 season, a couple of things happened: The Express didn't win any more with Steve Young than they had with their previous, much more affordable quarterback; Oldenburg's financial position turned out to be far less than he had touted; and he stopped paying his team's bills. So, by the summer of 1984, the USFL was looking for a new owner. That's why Max thought it might make sense for me.

My dream had always been to own a baseball team. But I was trying to use the resources God had put in my life. He'd blessed me with a relationship with Rick Hendrick, who had made my pursuit of a professional sports team possible financially and relationally. It was his friendship with Max Muhleman that made me think something might be possible. But I also realized that, while God may have blessed me with the financial resources and relationships to actually own a team, I still needed a lot more help.

I had no idea what owning a team would mean practically. Plus, the USFL's recent experience with Oldenburg had proven that simply having money (or just appearing to) doesn't mean a team will be successful. Moreover, I didn't just want to own a team; I wanted to have a successful franchise. I wanted to bring something to Charlotte that would transform the city, maybe even the state. So, on Max's advice, I decided to fly out to Los Angeles, just to educate myself. I might have owned a collection of business schools, but when it came to being a professional sports owner, I had a lot to learn.

In some ways, I felt a bit like Noah. God told him that a flood was coming, and people thought he was crazy. But he went about the business of preparing for the flood anyway. He had to get the cypress wood, he had to build it according to the specific dimensions God had given him, and then he had to go out and collect all the animals. Noah didn't care what other people said; he went out in obedience to God and made preparations. That's what I was trying to do. I was preparing.

But I didn't need to collect wood or animals; I needed to collect knowledge—and I realized God had already put people in my life to help me acquire it.

I took a number of people with me, including Charles Ricks, the accountant who had told me to get into the car business. I had a team of other financial analysts and lawyers with me as well. I might be from Charlotte, but we had lawyers out there too. I also took some of my top salespeople, because I knew, whether it was a car, a business school, or a football team, you still needed to *sell* it.

My one condition for going was that I didn't want any press. The whole thing needed to be confidential because I didn't want to deal with any speculation in the media. So, we got out there and were given a tour of the facility, watched a practice, talked with the people who worked there, and tried to learn as much as possible about the way a football team is run. I thought the trip was a success . . . until I learned that my request for no media coverage hadn't been adhered to.

When we got back, I saw the blurb in the *Los Angeles Times* about my trip and possible interest in the team. I know that the *Times* is a major newspaper on the West Coast, but the coverage couldn't have been ruder. They called me a hillbilly and basically made it out that this guy George Shinn, from North Carolina, was walking around with a straw hat on and piece of hay in his teeth, looking to buy himself a football team.

It wasn't nice or flattering. Even worse, it was public.

We were traveling on a private airplane, and when we landed in Charlotte, we were greeted by a bank of lights. The local media was all over the story and, by extension, me.

"Mr. Shinn, Mr. Shinn!" the reporters yelled. "What are you going to do? Are you buying the Los Angeles Express and moving them to Charlotte?"

"No, no. Nothing like that," I replied. "I am interested in a professional sports team. But I'm not going to buy that. I just won't. I'm learning the business. I'm educating myself."

Well, that didn't do much to dampen enthusiasm. After that, I couldn't really go anywhere in Charlotte without a reporter asking me whether a professional team was headed our way.

In a way, it was humbling. People were so hungry for something to come to our community. I believe it was partly to help elevate our city's status nationally and partly to help elevate our *people's* status nationally. I could tell the community was relying on me, and I didn't want to let them down.

In another way, it was incredibly gratifying. People were counting on me, but they were also looking at me. As my perceived responsibility to deliver something big for the city grew, so did my pride.

The USFL owners wanted me to come to Donald Trump's New York office to talk about the next steps. I was thinking about the idea of bringing an expansion team to Charlotte. The USFL seemed to add or subtract teams fairly frequently, so it seemed quite doable.

I went to New York and met with executives from the USFL and some league owners in one of the conference rooms of Trump Tower. One of the few people who wasn't there for the meeting was Trump himself—at least at first. As I talked with the owners of the Tampa Bay Bandits and the new Memphis franchise about the possibility of a new franchise in Charlotte, the door opened suddenly. In like a bolt of lightning came Donald Trump.

With his trademark haircut and New Yorker's bravado, he naturally cut an imposing figure. But the energy he brought to this meeting was also quite notable. Let's just say his language was different from how the folks talked at my local church back in Charlotte. He had a few things on his agenda that day. One was trying to convince the other owners to sue the NFL in an attempt to force them to merge with the USFL.

"In order for that to work," he said, "we need to move our games to the fall. That way we are direct competition, and they'll have to merge."

The other item for him was getting me to buy a team.

"Shinn, you need to buy the Express. It'll make you a lot of money!" he said.

John Bassett, the owner of the Bandits, could sense I was unsure. "Why don't you host an exhibition game to see how the market does?" he suggested as he pulled me aside. "I'm not sure buying into the league now makes sense, given the uncertainty. This will be a nice first step."

Well, I didn't like the idea of doing just one exhibition. Anyone will come to one game. If I had been invited to the Rose Bowl, for example, I would have gone no matter what. It was a onetime event. The test, to me, was seeing if people would come back. So, I left that meeting without buying the LA team, but I did agree to schedule *two* USFL preseason exhibition games for February 1985.

Max and I went about the business of generating excitement and community support for the game. I had invited the governors of both North Carolina and South Carolina to come, plus Charlotte's mayor. Between the appeal of the game and what it might mean to Charlotte in terms of possibly becoming a professional sports town, I thought we would have a good turnout. Then the day of the game arrived, and I woke up and looked at the sky.

Let's just say I felt like Noah again.

The skies were almost black, and the rain might as well have been biblical. It was cold, but not cold enough to snow. My first attempt to bring professional sports to Charlotte had been met with a cold, rainy day.

God help us, I thought as I looked out my window that morning.

He did.

Despite the weather, we still had more than sixteen thousand people in the twenty-three-thousand-seat grandstands of Charlotte's Memorial Stadium to watch Donald Trump's New Jersey Generals play the Memphis Showboats, the closest team to us geographically.

Former Heisman Trophy–winner Herschel Walker scored a touchdown for the Generals, while former University of Tennessee standout Reggie White suited up for Memphis. The crowd, under blankets and ponchos, cheered enthusiastically the entire time. Harry Usher, the USFL commissioner, addressed the crowd from the fifty-yard line, saying, "I am impressed!" over the loudspeaker.

Really, there was only thing that didn't go as I had hoped. The New Jersey Generals had long been rumored to be close to signing Doug Flutie, the former Heisman Trophy–winning quarterback for Boston College. Partly because, at five feet ten inches, he was short for a quarterback, and partly because he had thrown a famous Hail Mary pass to beat Miami in college, Flutie was a real fan favorite. I had hoped to bring him to Charlotte to throw a Hail Mary pass to a group of underprivileged children as part of the pregame festivities. I thought the kid who caught the pass could get free tickets to the next game.

Sadly, I was told that, since he hadn't technically signed with the Generals, they couldn't make him travel with the team.

"That's okay," I said. "I'll pay him $10,000 of my own money, bring him down and back in a private jet, and he can wear jeans and a T-shirt. I think the crowd would love it."

I *still* think the crowd would have loved it, but we couldn't get Doug Flutie's agent to agree, so he ended up not coming. Either way, the game was a hit, and the next one was even better. The following week we had the Baltimore Stars play the Tampa Bay Bandits, which were led by head coach Steve Spurrier. This time, the sky was sunny and the temperature was in the midsixties.

We sold out the entire stadium.

The fans were just as involved as they had been for the previous week's game. Hundreds of them brought signs that said, "WE WANT A FRANCHISE!"

I did too.

The success of the event and the amount of press it generated seemed to spur a lot of momentum for Charlotte's viability as a professional sports city. In fact, we proved to be more viable than the USFL itself.

In August 1984, six months before our exhibition games, the league's owners voted, in agreement with Donald Trump, to move the league's games to the fall starting in 1986. Not long after our exhibition games, the USFL filed an antitrust suit against the NFL. The unrest caused by the decision proved to be as crippling to the USFL as the eventual lawsuit. The following year, after a trial, a jury found that the NFL had violated antitrust provisions . . . but awarded the USFL only one dollar in damages. It was a devastating blow for the viability of the league.

By that time, it had become clear to me that the USFL, with its frequent expansions and contractions, wasn't the sort of stable sports league I wanted to be a part of. More importantly, it wasn't the type of thing I could be proud to bring to Charlotte.

However, I did feel like I was getting closer to my goal. I had met with owners, been asked to buy into a league, and even brought professional football to Charlotte—for two weeks, anyway. The boat was coming together. I just didn't know what kind of ship it would be—or what kind of voyage God would take me on.

CHAPTER 10

My Hail Mary from Half Court

The success of the USFL exhibitions had raised Charlotte's profile—and my own. The first game was so successful that the governor of North Carolina came to the second game. I had also recently sold my chain of business schools for the tidy sum of $35 million. So, feeling like I had made it to another level both professionally and financially, I wondered if this might be the time to pursue my ultimate dream of owning a baseball team.

Maybe now was the time to talk to Major League Baseball. One of the people I had met through my pursuit of a USFL team was friend Eddie Einhorn, who also was one of the owners of the Chicago White Sox. He offered to introduce me to Bobby Brown, one of the top officials with MLB. I liked the idea that God had led me to the USFL and that this path might also lead to major league baseball.

A four-time World Series champion as third baseman for the New York Yankees, Bobby Brown had retired from baseball, worked as a medical doctor, and then returned to the game, this time as president of the American League. Bobby was an incredibly smart and kind man. When I called him, I was direct and honest.

"Bobby, I'd give anything to own a baseball team," I told him. He certainly understood. In fact, he probably heard it all the time. "The problem is," I continued, "I don't know if I can afford one."

Bobby couldn't have been more helpful. He told me to come to New York with a financial statement that we could review together to see where I stood.

So, Max Muhleman and I headed to New York. My experience visiting out west to talk about football made me leery of heading to a strange place, where I might feel like I didn't belong.

When Max and I got there, Bobby was honest, but not in the way those lawyers and accountants had been. There was genuine care and hope in his voice.

"You're not strong enough, on your own, to buy a baseball team right now," he told me. "But I have a recommendation for you. A couple of team owners are actually *co-owners*. They own part of the team, and they even have less money than you do."

I have to admit, while not originally a fan of co-owner-ship, the model had worked quite successfully for me with Rick Hendrick and the car dealerships. And if it meant I could be an owner of a baseball team, I was certainly open to it.

However, it turned out that wasn't really an option either—at least not at that time.

"We don't have anyone looking to sell a stake right now," Bobby continued. "But if you're willing to wait, I will let you know when something comes up, because it happens all the time."

Bobby then took me to see the commissioner of baseball, a man named Peter Ueberroth. Ueberroth had been the chairman of the Los Angeles Olympics and set a record by turning the first privately financed Olympic games into a source of enormous profit. If I was going to become a baseball owner, I thought Ueberroth and I should get to know each other.

I told him I had grown up loving baseball and that while I was open to buying a minority stake, my real goal, and lifelong dream, was to get a professional baseball team for Charlotte.

Peter's advice was in line with Bobby's. But he was even more honest.

"Charlotte is too small," he told me. "Maybe in twenty-five or thirty years it might be big enough to host a baseball team. But you have to remember that baseball's season is one hundred and sixty-two games long. That means you're hosting eighty-one games a year. With the size of Charlotte's population, there's no way you can have enough people come out that often to make it work."

I was disappointed, but I understood his thinking. But then he said something that made me glad I'd taken the trip to New York.

"You know what you should be doing?" he said as he paused. "You should be talking to the NBA. You're in North Carolina right? That's basketball country. NBA Commissioner David Stern is looking for people to buy expansion franchises right now."

Sitting there in the baseball commissioner's office, a light came on. I hadn't thought about bringing a basketball franchise to the area, but just because it hadn't been my plan didn't mean it wasn't God's. I had come to New York because I felt like I was being led to buy a professional sports team. That's why I was in that room in the first place. I had pursued a football team, but that didn't work out. I was being told no by the baseball commissioner. But I wasn't just being told no. I was being told, "Look at basketball."

So I did.

"Well, thank you for that feedback," I told Commissioner Ueberroth. "You wouldn't happen to know where the NBA offices are, would you?"

It turns out he did. Peter Ueberroth gave me directions on how to walk there, and it wasn't that far away. After thanking the commissioner and Bobby Brown for their time, Max and I headed out on foot, down the streets of New York, toward the offices of the National Basketball Association.

It was easy enough to find, just as I had been told.

I walked in the front door and went up to the young woman working behind the desk.

She looked up from her desk. "Can I help you?" she asked cheerily.

"Yes ma'am, I sure hope so," I said. "I'm here to see David Stern."

"Well, do you have an appointment?" she asked.

"No, I don't. But my name is George Shinn. I understand you all are expanding, and I'd like to buy an expansion team."

"Okay, Mr. Shinn," she said, not really sure what to do. "And you don't have an appointment?"

"No ma'am, I don't. But I was just meeting with the commissioner of Major League Baseball, and he suggested I come speak to you. So, here I am."

She picked up the phone to make a call. "Why don't you have a seat. Someone will be with you in a minute."

The next thing I knew, a deputy commissioner named Russ Granik was making his way toward me.

"I hear you're interested in buying an expansion team?" he asked me.

"Yes, sir. I am."

"Great. For what city?" he asked.

"Charlotte," I told him proudly.

He paused for a minute. And I'm dead serious when I tell you the next words out of his mouth were, "Where's Charlotte?"

I happily filled him in on the magical place that was the great state of North Carolina. And without even meaning to, I started selling him on Charlotte . . . and on me.

I told him how I grew up near there, how wonderful it is, how great the people are. I told him about my background and how I'd made some money. Then I told him that I would give anything to have a team. Either he liked enough of what he heard or he thought other people in the office would get a kick out of the country boy who thought he could buy his way into the NBA. Either way, he took us back and introduced me to another NBA lawyer named Gary Bettman, who years later would run the National Hockey League.

Suddenly, I was in a second conference room on the same day, talking to commissioners of a different sport. The path I started down had brought me there. I had to see where it led.

Max and I sat there, answering many of the same questions Bobby Brown and Peter Ueberroth had asked us just hours before. It was almost like the meeting with the baseball offi-cials had been God's way of preparing me for this meeting. I'm halfway convinced that they had a speaker in that room and that the NBA commissioner at the time, David Stern, was listening to us in his office. Because, after a while, he burst into the room with a cigar in his mouth. It was kind of like Donald Trump. What is it with New Yorkers walking into rooms like that?

Unlike Trump, though, Stern wasn't telling me what I should do. He was asking me questions. He took his cigar out of his mouth, pointed it at me, and asked, "George, where is Charlotte?"

After meeting with the baseball officials, I knew how to answer that.

I told David that Charlotte was a regional sports market with a rich history of college basketball that, unlike New York or Los Angeles, didn't have any professional sports teams. What I think Stern understood was that, while we didn't have any other professional franchises that would have helped to demonstrate our pedigree as a market capable of supporting a team, it also meant the NBA wouldn't have any competition.

I told the group that we had more than four million fans who lived within an hour's drive of our new coliseum.

Stern nodded his head approvingly.

We spent about two hours with David Stern, Russ Granik, and Gary Bettman, with David and me doing most of the talking. Like the baseball execs, the basketball people didn't say yes, but they didn't say no either. They told us how the NBA was planning on expanding to several more cities and that the cost of a new franchise would be at least $20 million. If I was serious about applying, they said, I would need to fill out an in-depth application, then prove to the twenty-three NBA owners that we could sell season tickets—lots of tickets. We had to do all that before the NBA would decide to give us a franchise.

David Stern finally looked at me and was totally honest. "George, you're going to have to write a check for $100,000 just to apply," he said. "Can you do that?"

"Yes, sir. I can do that," I replied.

I actually *did not* know for sure if I could do that.

I might have been worth $35 million, but I'd never written a check for that much money before. So, I did the next best thing I could think of.

I took the application and, with all the audacity I could muster, told Stern, "Let me take this home and get to work on it. But you'll get your check."

I went home and began figuring out how in the heck I was going to be able to wrangle up the support—financial, emotional, and otherwise—to give us a viable chance at landing a team.

The first thing I knew was that I needed to get more investors than just Rick Hendrick. I met with John Georgius, the COO of First Union Bank, one of the largest banks in Charlotte. Within fifteen years, they would become Wachovia, which then would become Wells Fargo. While they were focused on growing their financial portfolio, John didn't see basketball as an asset he wanted to invest in. But he did introduce me to a yacht and race car investor named Felix Sabates. Felix had already been involved with professional sports in Charlotte when he helped bring in the now-defunct World Football League. He had also been involved with professional soccer in the area. I met with a broadcast executive named Cy Bahakel, who agreed to come on board as well. Cy's career had been in radio, and he had built a broadcast network across the Midwest and Southeast from scratch. With a net worth greater than Rick Hendrick, Felix Sabates, and me combined, Cy was very interested in the broadcast rights for an NBA team.

With all the investors lined up, we needed to drum up support in the community.

The good news was that we had the media on our side. After the coverage of the USFL games, I had proven to be someone who could get things done. Once people found out we were trying to bring an NBA team to Charlotte, it was in the local news all the time. That press coverage led to many speaking invitations from community groups about our plan.

It's a miracle I didn't gain too much weight at that time, because I literally couldn't tell you how many chicken dinners I ate while speaking to civic groups or clubs. Basically, my rule was, if the event was within driving distance, I would come. Some people asked what I charged to come speak. I told them I didn't charge anything. "I'll even pay for my own meal," I told them. I didn't need compensation for speaking or free food. I just wanted as many people as possible to get on board because I knew we needed as many ticket sales as possible.

One night, I was speaking to a civic group in Gastonia, a suburb of Charlotte. I was introduced by a well-dressed young woman who looked more like the kind of person you expect to see at a Rotary event than a basketball game.

I addressed the group as I normally did and emphasized how our games were going to be events that were family friendly and would help Charlotte build a national profile.

After my speech, while the crowd cheered, the well-dressed woman came back up to the stage and addressed the crowd.

"Mr. Shinn, that was an incredible speech," she exclaimed. "I don't know anything about basketball. I've never even been to a high school game. But if you get a team, I'm going to buy season tickets to your games."

With support from the community coming along nicely, I needed to get the backing of the local government officials. After all, this plan would be contingent on playing games in an arena that hadn't been built yet.

To begin the conversation, I addressed the city council and updated them on my plans.

One of the men who was helping lead the meeting was former mayor John Belk. Now, John Belk was from an old Charlotte family that was incredibly wealthy. The family was behind the department stores that carried their name, among other ventures. He was considered a "blue blood" of the town. I was sort of the opposite. My lack of status was made pretty well known when John called me up to speak that night.

After listening to countless citizens talk at the city council meeting about everything from how often their trash gets picked up to the local millage rate, it was finally my turn.

But Belk made it sound like, rather than this exciting up-and-coming movement that was going to permanently alter the city of Charlotte, it was about to be Redneck Story Time.

"We got a guy here from Kannapolis, up the road a little ways," Belk began. "He's a good old country boy who thinks he's going to bring an NBA team to Charlotte. Come on up here, George, and tell them your story."

Well, I had been sitting there for the entire meeting, and the longer the meeting took, with all the agenda items and different speakers they had, the more nervous I got. I can't really explain it, but when Mayor Belk called my name, I swear I thought I was going to collapse right then and there. I tried to stand up, but my legs wouldn't work. They were trembling, and could barely support my weight, which wasn't that much.

Mayor Belk even looked over at one point and said, "George, are you all right?"

I did my best to stand and steady myself as I made my way to the podium. But I could barely keep it together. It was the oddest thing that, after I'd given so many speeches to so many groups, this moment, in front of these important civic leaders, my body decided to fail me. In hindsight, I think it was God reminding me of where true authority lay. Yes, these people were in charge of the city of Charlotte, but God is in charge of His entire kingdom. And Charlotte was just a tiny speck in the galaxy that exists under God's sovereignty. Either way, with my physical body failing, all I could do was close my eyes and say a quick prayer.

As the things I did became greater in the eyes of the world, there's no doubt that my relationship with the ruler of the heavens and earth began to suffer. But I will never forget, in that moment, being humbled enough to know that the only way I was going to get through it was with God's help.

"God, please be with me," I said. "Don't let me mess this up." Suddenly, I could feel my heart rate slowing down, and my hand, which had been shaking as I fumbled for notes, steadied.

With God's help, a number of the skeptical leaders got on board, and we started a conversation about what it would look like to use the new arena for the team.

After the city council agreed to give us free use of the arena, I knew we were ready to bring our application and entry fee back to the NBA. But when I arrived in New York this time, I didn't wander in unannounced. I rented limousines, made sure the media knew we were coming, and brought North Carolina governor Jim Martin and Charlotte mayor Harvey Gantt with me. We also had several state troopers, fully armed, accompanying us. They were working security detail for Governor Martin, but I thought it added a nice touch. It looked like they were protecting our check.

Once we arrived at the NBA headquarters and stepped out of the limousines, throngs of reporters, mostly from the Carolinas, were there to ask us questions and cover our entrance. I think seeing how much the local media cared made an impression on the NBA.

So, too, did the research we had done.

Upon presenting the check and application to David Stern, I told the NBA officials that Charlotte being a single-team market was actually a good thing. Sure, our population might be smaller than other cities that already had pro teams and wanted more, but you can't measure a market by its size alone. Our research had shown that you have to look at other things in the area *besides* the people. The fact that we didn't have any other professional teams competing with us meant our fans had more available dollars than any other market. We had more available corporate dollars since Charlotte had a booming financial sector, but those companies had no high-profile place to spend their ad dollars. Those banks and financial firms would all buy corporate suites and sponsorship packages. We also talked about the enthusiasm of our fans. Nothing breeds passion like college basketball, and our area was filled with people who had proven to be crazy for the sport.

Commissioner Stern accepted our application and the check. He thanked Governor Martin for the time. And he looked at me and smiled.

"Nice job, George," he said. "Now, get ready. You've got to convince the rest of the owners now."

The rest of the owners were meeting the following month at their annual convention in Phoenix, Arizona. I knew the meeting would take place in a hotel conference room, like so many I'd been to before. But in my mind, it would be like going into the lions' den. And like Daniel, I knew I'd need all the help from God I could get.

CHAPTER 11
God's Slam Dunk for Charlotte

Writing to the emerging Christian church, the apostle John told believers in 1 John 5:14, "This is the confidence we have in approaching God: that if we ask anything according to his will, he hears us."

That's something I know to be true. However, as I continued my pursuit of a new NBA franchise, I didn't try everything I could think of to elevate my voice to God's ear.

Before the big board of governors meeting in Phoenix with all the NBA owners, I had to meet with members of the NBA's expansion committee in New York to present them with preliminary information as a follow-up to our application. To say I was nervous would be an understatement. Yes, I had turned in our paperwork and delivered our check with some pomp and circumstance to convey confidence. But in truth, I was terrified. I didn't know what I was doing, and I was afraid of letting down all the people back in Charlotte.

I was by myself in New York, getting ready for the meeting that day. I knew that, as much as the NBA officials were reviewing applications and looking at hard numbers about

Charlotte, our facilities, and our population, they were also looking at me. That's the part that made me nervous.

Yes, I'd had some success in business, but now I was trying to literally and figuratively enter the big leagues. Deep down, I still felt a bit like the kid who finished last in his high school class. But whenever I started to feel anxious, I remembered to let the Lord take over. If I was going to have any chance, I needed God. That was the only way this would work.

I knelt down in my hotel room, opened the window to let some air in, and started to pray to God. I was a big believer in praying out loud then, and I still am today. I believe in the power of using my real voice for God. I like to think of God as my partner, so I talk to Him out loud just like I would talk to anyone else.

I had a hard time hearing with the windows open, talking to God over the sounds of New York City's traffic below. Even though it was early in the morning, the sounds of all the car horns were drowning out my thoughts. In my silly mind, I thought they could be keeping God from hearing me too.

With the traffic showing no signs of quieting down, I decided to get closer to God the only way I knew how. I left my hotel and went looking for a church.

And I knew exactly where to go.

Two decades earlier, I had been driving down the interstate in my 1957 Corvette and looking for some music to listen to on the radio. That car had a unique feature called a Wonder Bar radio that automatically looked for a station with an incoming signal. There I was, on the road, looking for something that would entertain me. All of a sudden, this voice just started booming out of my speakers. It wasn't exactly like when I felt God on the side of the road when I was facing bankruptcy and losing my business, but when I heard the speaker's voice for the first time, I definitely felt God's presence.

When the program, which had been both enlightening and entertaining, was over, an announcer came on and said, "You have been listening to Dr. Norman Vincent Peale."

I was so captivated by the message and Dr. Peale's delivery that I immediately found his book, *The Power of Positive Thinking*, when I got home. It reinforced a great deal of what I had come to believe, and it helped me see things in an even clearer way. The more positively I started thinking, the more positive things happened in my life.

Eventually, I wrote Dr. Peale a letter, telling him how much his book had impacted me. "This book has changed my life," I wrote. "I'm going to buy all your books, and if I get the chance, I would love to meet you one day." I checked my mail every day for months, hoping for a response. It took a while, but I did eventually get a response. In a letter to me, Dr. Peale was incredibly uplifting, and he told me that he would like to meet me someday.

Unbelievably, I did get to meet Dr. Peale. I think he was so taken by my story, where I'd come from, and where God had taken me that Dr. Peale invested in me. He saw God's work in my life and wanted to encourage me to continue pursuing it. He became a mentor and a friend. Along with Lowell Thomas, the famous broadcaster, Dr. Peale nominated me for the Horatio Alger Award, given to someone who embodies a sort of "rags to riches" story like the characters in Horatio Alger's books.

I remember telling my mother that I'd been nominated for that award, but I didn't think I would win it.

"Why wouldn't you win it?" she marveled. "You've been nominated by Lowell Thomas and Dr. Peale! Of course you're going to win."

Once again, she was right.

I won that award at the age of thirty-four, the youngest person ever to do so, all thanks to Dr. Peale and Mr. Thomas.

Dr. Peale asked me to speak to groups he was a part of. He would introduce me by telling audiences, "He's the most incredible young man I've ever met in my life." He wanted me to talk about how I invited God to be my CEO and what had happened ever since.

Simply put, Dr. Peale saw God's work in me. But he also knew it could be better.

"You know you've got a great gift," he once told me. "You could be an excellent speaker. But there are things you'll need to get better at. You have a crutch."

"A crutch?" I repeated curiously. I didn't know what he was talking about. Since my teacher in school had helped me overcome my stuttering, I had taken a lot of pride in speaking clearly and quickly, not stammering or using "ums" as placeholders.

"Yes, a crutch," he insisted. "You use notes. I can see when you're looking at them, and an audience can see you looking at them. But when you talk from the heart, you don't need your notes."

Talking with no notes seemed like an impossible task. How could you convey so much information from just your head?

"It's actually pretty simple," Dr. Peale explained. "All you need to do is break your speech into three or four points. And then decide which story you'll tell for each point, and tie them in. So, instead of memorizing an entire speech, you just need to remember your four points, and then tell your stories from the heart after that."

I went home and thought about what he had said, though I never did get comfortable enough to give a speech without notes.

A little while later, Dr. Peale invited me to one of his seminars designed to help preachers across the United States. He asked me to tell my story to this group of people who were trying to spread God's message all over the country.

When I got to the ballroom where the speech would be, one of Dr. Peale's assistants brought me up to the podium on the stage, where the head table for the luncheon was also located.

"This is where you'll be speaking," he told me, pointing to the podium.

"Great," I replied. I placed my speech notes on the podium and looked around at the crowd filing in, sitting at the tables as lunch was being served. I sat down at the table where they told me to. The room continued to fill, and meals were eventually served.

But I didn't see Dr. Peale.

"Excuse me," I asked his assistant. "But do you know where Dr. Peale is?" I was starting to get a little nervous.

"Dr. Peale will be here when he's ready," the assistant said.

I continued to wait. All of a sudden, I heard people in the back of the ballroom stand up and begin to applaud. I looked up to see Dr. Peale walking through the crowd. He stopped at a riser in front of the stage. I saw a microphone stand on the platform as well. It was next to where I was sitting . . . not at the podium where I had placed my notes.

"Good morning, George, how are you doing?" Dr. Peale asked, smiling at me.

"I'm great, Dr. Peale. Good to see you."

Dr. Peale turned to the crowd and began addressing the pastors and their families from the riser.

"I want to introduce you to this young man who has an incredible story that can change your life," Dr. Peale told the crowd. "George, come on down here."

I got up and turned toward the podium behind the table to reach for my notes.

"George, come on down *here!*" Dr. Peale demanded.

I walked down to where Dr. Peale was, leaving my notes behind. Then I began speaking from memory, just as he told me to. The speech went terrifically. I couldn't believe it. After that, I never used notes again, thanks to Dr. Peale.

I would need to be just as eloquent and persuasive in my upcoming meetings with NBA executives. I needed the confidence that Dr. Peale—and God—had helped me find. I headed out to Dr. Peale's church in downtown New York to see if, in this moment of spiritual need, I could find that confidence again.

Built in the 1850s, the famous building is actually covered on the outside by Tuckahoe marble, which is how Marble Collegiate Church got its name. When I arrived at the corner of Twenty-Ninth and Fifth, I looked up to see a giant spire on top of the trademark Gothic architecture. But the outside would be the only thing I got to admire about the building. When I arrived at the steps of Dr. Peale's church, I was saddened and a little surprised to find that the doors were locked. It felt wrong. I was sure that inviting God into this time and space in my life was the right thing to do. And going to a church felt like the right place to do it.

I turned around and looked up, sort of asking, "Okay, God, what now?"

My eyes settled on another steeple just across the street. There was a Catholic church, and it looked like people were coming out.

I didn't know much about the Catholic church, so I was a little reluctant to even go in. I remember opening the door slowly, and I saw people lighting candles. I had no clue what that meant; I just knew I was looking for the Lord. And then . . . I found Him. Near the front, I saw a big statue of Jesus on the cross.

That's who I need to talk to, I thought.

I might have been in a different type of church than I was used to, but I was more comfortable than ever talking to Jesus that day.

"Lord," I started, "I am really scared. Please be with me today. I want so much for this to work. Nobody thinks I have a chance, and everybody thinks I'm crazy.

"The only way this will work is if You're involved. I need Your help. You've guided me this far and put people like Dr. Peale in my life to help me achieve Your vision. Please give me strength tomorrow, and please keep my leg from shaking like it did in that city council presentation in Charlotte. I can't do this by myself, but with You by my side, I know all things are possible. Amen."

The next day when I made my presentation, I didn't use any notes and my leg didn't shake. I was calm, and I felt like God was with me, giving me strength and projecting the kind of confidence that only a relationship with the Lord can provide.

The NBA officials told me everything looked good and that the next important step would be making our case to the entire league at the annual board of governors meeting, which would be later that year in Phoenix. There I would need to sell the league's owners on why Charlotte was worthy of a new franchise.

My wife, Carolyn, and I, along with my fellow owners, Rick Hendrick, Felix Sabates, and Max Muhleman, all came to

Phoenix for the meeting. It was a big affair, with an event the night before for all the prospective cities giving their pitches the next day.

It was sort of like being back in high school. We were the new kids in class, and we definitely didn't have any friends to sit with at lunch. The ownership group from Miami was incredibly popular. So was the group from Orlando. You could tell a lot of the owners liked the idea of spending more time at Disney World and South Beach. But I don't think they knew too much about Charlotte. Still, it was nice to be in the room with the people we hoped to join, and I think it was good to get a sense of the fact that, in the eyes of the owners, we weren't a priority.

But that was okay; it just made me want to work even harder. It was 10:00 p.m. by the time Carolyn and I got back to the room. She got ready for bed, and I got down to work. I got all my notes out and started practicing my pitch out loud, over and over. I knew what points I wanted to make and how I wanted to make them. I walked back and forth across the living room. Eventually, around midnight, Carolyn called out to me.

"George, are you coming to bed?" she asked, somewhat annoyed.

"No, I've got to get ready for tomorrow," I replied. I knew she understood how important this was to me . . . and to us.

Practicing my pitch was important. But so was sleep.

"Well, can you go practice in the bathroom and turn the lights out, please?"

Off to the bathroom I went. My journey to own a professional sports team had already taken me to some strange places. Now, it was taking me to a hotel bathroom—but that turned out to be a blessing in its own way. Looking in the bathroom

Me and Mom

Me, Mom, and Dad outside his gas station

Mom with our dog Pepe

A drawing given to us of Dad's gas station

Me (center) with two friends; I spent my
childhood in hand-me-down-clothes.

My sister Patsy, who is six years older, with our dog Sparky

Me and Magic Johnson

Me and Mayor Gantt riding in
a parade celebrating the birth
of the Charlotte Hornets

My partners Rick Hendrick and
Felix Sebates in the parade

Mayor Harvey Gantt and me at a press
conference announcing the Hornets

Pre-game with my favorite player, Muggsy Bogues

Muggsy is ever loved by Louie, our standard poodle

Me and Megan with Pat Boone

Me with Debbie Boone

When I received the Horatio Alger Award; I am on the left,
Arthur Godfrey is beside me, Danny Thomas is standing
behind us, and Norman Vincent Peale is at the podium.

Megan and me at the George Shinn Event
Center at Lipscomb University

I love speaking to audiences!

Megan and me with Franklin and Jane Graham in their office

Me and my brother Bobby, who was ten years
older and retired from the Air Force

A visit from my three children: Chad, Chris, and Susan

Chad and Susan came to visit on Father's Day.

Me and Megan on our wedding day

At our Cornerstone Christian Bookstore in North Carolina

My love, Megan

We donated a car that raised $1.76 million for
Franklin Graham's efforts in Ukraine.

Me with Rick Hendrick, one of the best business partners ever

mirror, I could practice and watch my facial expressions, which helped me home in on when to smile, when to look up, and when to pause with just the right look on my face.

I practiced literally all night. As the sun started coming up, I realized I needed both some fresh air and some coffee. I opened the door and was about to head out when I looked down and saw a newspaper on the welcome mat. It was laid flat, with the top half of the paper staring back at me. The big headline on page one read, "NBA IN TOWN."

"Yeah, buddy," I said to myself.

No longer worried about coffee, I brought the paper in to see what the coverage said about our chances. Sure enough, the writer had ranked the prospects of all eleven cities that were vying for a bid, since the NBA was expected to grant only three or four new franchises.

Number one on the list, in the opinion of the writer, was Minneapolis. I wasn't bothered by that. Minneapolis already had NFL, NHL, and MLB teams, and they even had an NBA team previously, before the Minneapolis Lakers moved to Los Angeles. The fact that they kept the name Lakers even though they moved from Minnesota—a state known for its ten thousand lakes—to Los Angeles never made sense to me.

My eyes kept scanning down the list to see where they ranked Charlotte. I had to look for a while.

Down at the very bottom of the list, ranked dead last, was Charlotte, North Carolina.

I'll never forget what the writer said about us. Since we were the smallest city in terms of population and had no existing professional sports franchise, we didn't get much respect.

"The only franchise Charlotte will get," the article said, "will be one with golden arches."

I was so upset. But at the same time, it added so much fuel to my tank and fired me up.

I definitely didn't need coffee anymore.

Although Rick, Felix, and Max had accompanied me to the meeting, I would be the only one speaking. As we walked down the hallway toward the meeting room, the anger inside me started to give way to nervousness. Before a big speech, my nerves usually make me need to use the bathroom.

You can imagine my surprise when, as I was in the restroom, I suddenly heard a noise, and then a voice, and saw bright lights suddenly shining from behind me.

I turned my head to see Harold Johnson, the sports reporter from Charlotte's Channel 9 news with a camera pointed at my face.

"Hey, George. How are you feeling about our chances?" he asked.

I appreciated Harold's enthusiasm for the story, if not his timing.

"Harold, I tell you what," I replied. "You cut that camera off, give me a minute and I'll be happy to talk to you. I feel great about our chances."

Channel 9 didn't run that clip on television, but I thought it was funny how I had practiced in an unusual location earlier and now was being interviewed in one too. Plus, I think having a lighthearted moment helped calm me down as well.

When it was our turn, we entered the ballroom where the owners had all assembled. It was exciting—and humbling— to be speaking to legendary NBA figures like Lakers owner Jerry Buss and Boston Celtics owner Red Auerbach. I said a quick prayer, once again asking God to help me, and I rose to begin.

I was glad that my legs seemed relatively still. It was almost like I was back on the side of the interstate outside Raleigh. I should have been nervous, but I had an inner peace in my soul and could feel God's presence by my side.

My presentation focused on three main points: our collective size was actually much larger than people thought, our local community was incredibly supportive with a tremendous capacity to demonstrate that support, and our fans were enthusiastic.

"Charlotte might be the smallest city in the NBA," I told the owners. "But you can't think of it as just Charlotte. You have to think of it as the Carolinas."

I told them Charlotte is right in the center of North and South Carolina. People drive from all over both states to come to Charlotte all the time. If you include both states, I said, we have a population of over four million people.

This got the group's attention.

Then, when I told the owners about our agreement with our new arena, they started to change the way they thought about Charlotte having an NBA team.

Before coming to Phoenix, I had met with Charlotte's new mayor, Harvey Gant. Harvey had been on the city council for ten years before being elected as Charlotte's first African American mayor. I told Harvey that he should lease us the new coliseum for one dollar a year. In return, we would give the city the revenues generated from the games held at the coliseum.

At first, Harvey's reaction was skeptical to say the least.

"George, if I do that, I'll be run out of office," he told me.

I disagreed.

"If you listen to me, and if you follow the plan, you'll be reelected," I told him.

What I laid out to him was simple. I showed him how, if the city leased us the building cheaply but made money on parking and food concessions, the city government would actually make way more money than it would on rent alone.

"Plus, if you lease me the arena for a high price, I can't get a team anyways and you won't make any money."

Harvey eventually agreed. When I told the owners what we secured the lease for, I was glad he had. Everyone in the room sat up when I told them we had our arena for a dollar a year.

No other owner in the league had a deal like that. Not even close.

The presentation was going well, and I was building to the final point. Our area was bigger than people thought. Our community was willing to support us in ways no other city would.

"And . . ." I said as I scanned the room. Everyone was looking at me. I paused for dramatic effect before continuing. "Our fans are literally lined up around the block to attend basketball games in North Carolina. We have, as of this date, presold ten thousand season tickets."

The NBA had told us presales would be a big factor in the decision on where to expand. I thought ten thousand season tickets was a lot, but when the owners jumped out of their seats and began applauding, I knew it was a monumental achievement.

Praise God!

After the presentation, individual owners came up to me and the rest of our ownership group with measurable enthusiasm. Red Auerbach gave me a hug and told me I'd done an amazing job.

Multiple owners told me they were rooting for Charlotte. That was nice to hear. But nothing was nicer than being able to silently and prayerfully thank God for His help in the peaceful quiet of the plane on the way home.

And I wasn't done talking to God.

The NBA told us they would announce their decision on, ironically, April 1. After the meetings in Phoenix, I was optimistic, but nothing was a sure thing.

I went to the office on April 1 determined to attend to other matters, trying to keep my mind off the NBA decision. David Stern had promised he would call that day with the decision, one way or another.

By 6:00 p.m., I hadn't heard anything and started to assume the worst. As I drove home, my thoughts became incredibly negative. More than thinking about God in that moment, I thought about myself. *How could I fail? How could I let all these people down?*

It was a terrible feeling.

When I got home and pulled into the garage, Chris, my older son, opened the door.

I love my son, but I didn't really want to see him at the moment. I was in too bad of a mood. I just wanted to sit there and yell and sulk, thinking about how little sleep I would probably get that night.

Eventually, Chris got tired of waiting and hollered out from the steps, "Dad! You got a call from David Stern. You need to get in here and call him back!"

Well, having already talked myself into the idea that the news was bad, I wasn't in any hurry. So, I sort of just kept sitting there.

"Dad!" Chris yelled again. "David Stern is the commissioner of the NBA!"

"Chris, I know who David Stern is," I replied. By this time, it was nearly 9:00 p.m. I knew a call this late couldn't be good news. And, truthfully, my pride didn't want anyone to see me cry when I got the bad news. So, with my head low, I went into my bedroom, sat down, and called the NBA.

A friendly young female voice answered the phone.

"Good evening, NBA."

"Ma'am, this is George Shinn, returning the commissioner's call."

"Hold on," she replied before putting me on hold.

Russ Granik, the deputy commissioner who was the first man I had spoken with in my initial trip to the league offices, picked up the phone.

"George, David's tied up right now. Do you want to hold or do you want him to call you back?"

At this point, I was sad, it was late, and I was sitting by myself, just wanting the conversation to be over with.

"Russ, why can't you just tell me what's going on?" I asked.

"David has to tell you," Russ replied sternly.

That didn't make me feel any better.

"No, I'm not gonna hang up," I told him. "I'll stay on the line."

I have no idea how long I was really on hold, but it felt like half an hour.

Eventually, I heard David's voice.

"George, this is David. I know today is April Fool's Day. But what I'm going to tell you is not an April Fool's joke. I'm calling you first," he said, "because you were picked first. Congratulations, and welcome to the NBA."

I was overwhelmed with an avalanche of emotions. I was happy, excited, scared, proud, and humbled.

But above all, I was thankful.

I knew God had done this. To some, it was just a sports team. But it was so much bigger than that. It was the latest improbable thing God had done in my life, despite my short-comings. I was so incredibly humbled to be part of His work.

"Thank you, Jesus!" I shouted.

To be fair, I also thanked David Stern.

"David, I'm going to make you proud," I said. "I promise you, you're going to be proud of me and what we do with this franchise."

It had been a long and winding road to get a professional sports franchise. It had taken me to California and New York, and it had made me think about possible ventures with foot-ball and baseball. But I believe God can do infinitely more in our lives than we ever thought possible.

He certainly has in mine.

CHAPTER 12

God's Pieces Come Together

The Old Testament book of Nehemiah tells a story I often thought of as I led the efforts to prepare Charlotte to launch our first NBA season.

The book of Ezra, which immediately precedes Nehemiah in the Bible, recounts Ezra's efforts to rebuild Jerusalem's holy temple nearly a century after the Babylonian army sacked the city. In the first chapter of Nehemiah, we learn that Nehemiah, a Jew, was serving as cupbearer to the king of Persia. Upon meeting some fellow Jewish travelers from Judah, Nehemiah learned that the walls of the city were still destroyed. He wept at the news.

The walls of Jerusalem were important for the city and are meaningful to us today in understanding what God calls us to do. While the temple was clearly a holy place where God was worshipped, the walls were meant to protect the city and the temple. The nicer the temple, the greater the need for walls to protect it.

Nehemiah felt called by God to go to Jerusalem and rebuild its city walls. To do that, he asked the king for time off from his job to go and do the work, and he asked for the king's protection as he made his journey. Because it was something that God blessed, Nehemiah got the help he needed. Nehemiah 2:9 tells us he had "army officers and cavalry" assisting him on his way.

Obviously, we were building a basketball team, not a city wall. And our team wasn't going to physically protect the city from threats of violence or destruction the way ancient city walls did. But, in some ways, I truly believed we were building something just as important.

Charlotte was about to be introduced to the rest of the country in a way it never had been before. Like Nehemiah, I felt God had called me to this journey and had blessed me every step of the way. Now, as my dream was becoming a reality, I, like Nehemiah, needed all the help I could get—whether it was officers, a cavalry, or just other people with expertise that I didn't have.

Some of it would prove to be more useful than others.

Something that made me successful early in my career was an ability to sell. I learned from my mother the value of the soft sell approach. I also learned, over time, the importance of marketing. So, my first thought when we were awarded the franchise was how we would present ourselves not just to our city but to the entire country.

We needed a name, jerseys, and a mascot.

Initially, I asked a group of local Charlotte elites, or what I used to call the "blue bloods," to help me come up with a name. I figured early buy-in from the movers and shakers of the city would help with other aspects of the team.

We had a meeting to decide on the team's name at a local television studio. After kicking around a few different ideas, I excused myself. When I came back, they had already made up their minds: they wanted to call the team the Spirit.

"The Spirit?!" I said. "Where'd you come up with that?"

The group's response was actually somewhat validating.

"Look, you accomplished this goal against all odds," the group said. "Nobody thought you'd do it. You ended up being picked first. The spirit of this city—and your spirit in particular—is what made this happen. So, we can be the Spirit."

I reluctantly agreed, and we announced that the team was the Spirit.

Let's just say not everyone was as positive as the group. The press coverage the next day was overwhelmingly negative. One sportswriter, the famous columnist Tom Sorensen, wrote, "What's Shinn's mascot going to be? Casper the Friendly Ghost?"

The response was humiliating.

Instead of letting my pride get in the way, I was able to admit the name was a mistake.

I decided to let the community decide by voting on whether they liked the name Spirit compared to other options, including Hornets, Knights, Cougars, and a few others. The fans overwhelmingly chose Hornets, which, while technically an insect, also referred to Charlotte's reputation of being the "hornet's nest of the American Revolution."

The name was locked in. Now, we needed jerseys and a mascot.

For the jerseys, my partner Max knew a famous clothing designer named Alexander Julian from Chapel Hill, North Carolina. I was always a big fan of his clothing line, and he had won several awards for doing unique things with traditional menswear. Between his advice to me in my pursuit of the franchise and his connections that got us our designer for our jersey, Max's fingerprints were on every part of what the Hornets would become. And it's a good thing they were.

As we were about to present our city to the country, I loved the idea of having something fashionable. People thought North Carolina was the country, but we had class too.

I was concerned about Julian's price though. I mean, fashion can be expensive.

Thankfully, God helped work out a deal.

I asked Julian, who was quite successful and wealthy at the time, if I could afford him.

His response was gracious but also problematic.

"George, I would be honored to design the uniforms for free," he said. "But if you sell copies of them, then I would like my standard 5 percent royalty."

"I don't think I can do that," I said. "In this league, everything is all shared revenue, and I don't think I can do a carve out like that."

Luckily, I had a counteroffer that was much more workable.

"I'll tell you what," I said. "You give me ownership of the design for five pounds of Carolina barbecue a month."

Now, that might seem like asking for an incredible concession on his part. And, in truth, it was. But in North Carolina, we jokingly call our barbecue *Carolina Caviar*. We are proud of it.

"George, you've got yourself a deal!" he said.

Years later, when asked by a writer to describe the experience of his deal with us, Alexander had a great line.

"Well, George got rich, and I got fat," he said. "I traded $10 million worth of royalties for a gut."

It was, in fact, a great deal for the city of Charlotte, because Alexander Julian came up with one of the most iconic designs in sports.

His signature colors were teal and purple, so I sent him a couple of samples I liked that I thought were close to that. He called me up one day and said that what I thought was teal was more of a forest green.

"My signature color is more of a blue-green, George," he explained.

"Well, that's fine, but our arena is going to be teal, so our jerseys should be too," I countered.

"I know your architects have chosen this for your stadium," he said. "But your uniforms are not going to be that color. They're going to be my teal. The reason I use it for fashion, along with purple, is that it looks good on everybody. All skin colors look great in teal or in purple. There's a wide range of skin colors in the NBA. It enhances everybody at the same time. I promise you won't regret it."

I have to say I thought his answers were compelling. We went with teal. And, decades later, I'm glad he held his ground. Our jerseys weren't just popular in the NBA; they led an entire fashion movement in the country. The teal color became the go-to look, and several new sports franchises would adopt a similar color scheme within the next few years.

Julian not only designed our jerseys but also played a key role in our mascot's design. I asked him to tell me the best person in the world to design our mascot. We had a world-class designer for our jerseys, and I wanted our mascot to be just as good.

"That's easy," he told me. "Get Jim Henson."

Famous for creating the Muppets characters and many other adorable animal figures, getting Jim Henson was a genius idea. Julian knew him and personally called him to ask about designing our mascot. Henson said he was interested, but he wanted to keep the rights to the mascot.

I quickly found out from the NBA that I wasn't allowed to make that arrangement.

I got his number from Julian and called Jim Henson myself. "What if I pay you double?" I countered. More money never hurt. I also mentioned all the publicity we would be getting with the launch of the new team and the publicity Alexander Julian got when he designed our uniforms.

"You would get just as much publicity as he did. And I'll pay you double what I paid Julian for the design," I offered.

I meant, of course, about ten pounds of barbecue. But he didn't know that.

Either way, I think he could tell I wasn't going to give up.

"How about this," he finally said. "My daughter is joining our team, and if you work with her, while I oversee the project, we have a deal."

And that's how Cheryl Henson ended up designing the costume of Hugo the Hornet. Hugo would become an iconic fixture associated with not only our team but our city.

Our wall was coming together.

Once we had our mascot and uniform design figured out, we had to focus on something equally important: who would be *wearing* those teal beauties on the court.

I sat down with Felix Sabates and asked, "Can you believe we are NBA owners?"

"Yeah. That's what we signed up for, isn't it?" he said matter-of-factly. He wasn't wrong. But after my journeys to meet with football owners and baseball commissioners, plus conversations I had with current NBA owners, I had learned one thing: you need to have people around you who really know the game.

"Felix," I said, "I've been thinking. Do you know much about basketball?"

In his classic way, Felix replied, "No, and neither do you, and neither does anybody else. We'll have to bring in somebody who knows what he's doing."

David Stern suggested we reach out to a man named Carl Scheer.

Carl had been involved in professional basketball for nearly two decades as the general manager for different NBA and ABA teams and also as the commissioner of the rival Continental Basketball Association. More than just experience with running a basketball team, though, he knew what fans wanted. When he was with the Denver Nuggets, he was the one who suggested having a slam dunk contest during the American Basketball Association's All-Star Game. I liked that he was innovative while also being experienced. Plus, he didn't have a problem with me being part of the day-to-day operations.

So, we hired Carl to be our first general manager. He took the lead on helping us hire a coach and began scouting to fill out our roster. I was still heavily involved though. When we interviewed candidates for our first coach, for example, I was there for every interview. We looked at a wide assortment of possibilities.

One person we didn't get to interview was NBA legend "Pistol" Pete Maravich. He had called me out of the blue in late 1987, telling me he would really like to get into coaching and asked if I would consider him for an interview.

"We aren't ready to hire a basketball coach yet," I told him, explaining that we were still filling out the administrative and sales side of the operation. "But when we get ready, I will definitely give you an interview."

"That's all I ask," he told me. We exchanged numbers, and I really thought he would make an excellent coach. Unfortunately, he died suddenly just two months later, at the age of forty. It was a tragedy, and I'm sorry I never got to meet him and give him the interview I promised.

But we gave interviews to a lot of other candidates.

We interviewed Larry Brown, who played at North Carolina, had been an assistant under Dean Smith, and had just won a national title at Kansas. He was obviously a skilled coach, had been in the NBA before, and would go on to have an outstanding career and win a title with the Detroit Pistons. When we spoke to him, Carl asked him point-blank if he thought he could handle losing the amount of games we, as an expansion franchise, would probably lose. He candidly said no. So, we thanked him for his time and moved on. He accepted a job coaching the San Antonio Spurs later that spring.

We also spoke with Boston Celtics legend Tommy Heinsohn and Gary Williams, who was the coach at Ohio State. Neither seemed to have the kind of temperament we were looking for.

Finally, Carl arranged an interview with Dick Harter, who'd been an assistant with the Indiana Pacers. I was impressed with his preparation, organization, and, to be honest, his attire. He wore a tie and jacket, and based on our conversation, I knew him to be a man of God who read the Bible. I liked him immediately and ultimately offered him the job.

With our general manager and coach in place, we got ready for the expansion draft, in which new teams pick from the reserve players of all the other teams in the league. Each team can protect eight players on their roster, and we got the picks, along with the Miami Heat, of everyone else.

The Miami Heat won the coin flip, so they had the top pick. With our first pick, the second overall pick of the expansion draft, Carl felt strongly that a shooting guard from the Cleveland Cavaliers named Dell Curry would be a great player for us. As it turns out, he was right. Dell would be an amazing player for us over the next decade.

Carl and Coach Harter had ideas about what players would work, but there was one player I wanted more than anyone: a point guard named Muggsy Bogues, who had been left unprotected by the Washington Bullets.

Muggsy was from Baltimore originally, but he had played college basketball at Wake Forest University, just up the road from Charlotte in Winston-Salem. He was more than a popular local player; he was someone I knew our fans could relate to—because he was only five foot three. He was literally the only player in the NBA who was shorter than me.

Obviously, basketball is a tall man's game. In fact, one of Muggsy's teammates on the Bullets was a seven-foot-seven player named Manute Bol. So, the previous season, the Bullets had both the tallest and shortest players in the league on the same team—and they made the playoffs with them. I saw Muggsy's inclusion as a way of appealing to the fans who could relate to a player who was closer to their size while still giving the Hornets a talented, experienced player who knew how to win.

Not everyone was excited about the idea of having such a small player on our team. First and foremost was our coach, who didn't want us to pick Muggsy.

"He's way too short," Coach Harter said. "He's not tall enough to rebound or defend anyone who goes up for a jump shot. As an expansion team, we are going to have a hard enough time without being handicapped like that."

Dick was an old-school coach, and I respected his approach, pedigree, and opinion.

But I still wanted to draft Muggsy Bogues.

I thought having a more relatable player would help with ticket sales, and frankly, I loved the way he played. He was like a lightning bolt on the court; he played with an energy and relentlessness I thought would excite the crowd and inspire a similar level of play from his teammates.

I also couldn't help but feel a sort of kinship with him. Like me, he was an underdog. At his size, he had no business being in the NBA. But against all odds, he had worked hard, been opportunistic, and had excelled. I loved that.

As a short player, he might not have been able to shoot over others, but he could use the natural gifts God had given him— his quickness and an unselfish spirit—to help others succeed. And while some thought his diminutive stature was a weakness, he found a way to see it as a blessing. He used the fact that others couldn't see him to his advantage, sneaking up behind others and taking the ball from them. He had even finished his career at Wake Forest as the all-time leader in the Atlantic Coast Conference in steals and assists.

I didn't love the idea of going against the man I had hired to coach my team, but I also couldn't help being drawn to this player who checked so many boxes. I had identified with the David versus Goliath scenario for so much of my life. How could I overlook a chance to get a player who seemed to be made from that mold as well?

I called Dean Smith, who was practically a five-star general of college coaches. He was the legendary head coach at the

University of North Carolina, which was in the same conference as Wake Forest, and coached against Muggsy for four years.

"Would you pick Muggsy?" I asked Coach Smith. "What
does he do well, and what doesn't he do? Can he help my team?"

Coach Smith didn't hesitate.

"Whenever we played Wake Forest," he began, "I always
told my players that if they couldn't see Muggsy, that if he was
not in their line of sight, they were to hold the ball high in the
air. Because if they didn't, I knew he was going to take it away
from them."

Coach Smith concluded, "Muggsy is a menace. And he's
relentless."

To me, the respect one of the legends of basketball had for
Muggsy Bogues was all I needed to hear.

"Thank you, Coach Smith," I told him. "We're going to
pick Muggsy."

I told Carl Scheer and Dick Harter.

And, as the owner, I won the argument.

We drafted Muggsy with the sixth overall pick in the expansion draft. A few weeks later, after the rookie draft, we had the
rest of our roster assembled.

There was a palpable buzz in the city for the Hornets. As
the first game approached that fall, I prayed that the "wall" we
were building would glorify God. I was confident His hand
had been in it. Now I just needed to get out of the way.

I was grateful for the people and resources He had given
me in this journey. As I had remarked to Felix in a conversation
earlier, I really didn't know what I was doing. But I was trusting
God was putting the pieces around me to make sure it reflected
the city, us, and Him in the right way.

We had our jerseys. We had our team. We had our wall.

We felt ready to present and defend our city to the rest of the world. And we prayed that God would continue to be with us as we did it.

CHAPTER 13
Dying for a Win

One common tenet from Jesus's teaching is the concept of dying to yourself. It's a message Jesus repeatedly told to a variety of audiences. When He was healing, performing miracles, and speaking to large crowds, He had one message that largely revolved around keeping God at the center of your life.

The most important commandment, Jesus said more than once, including in Matthew's Gospel, is "'Love the Lord your God with all your heart and with all your soul and with all your mind.' This is the first and greatest commandment. And the second is like it: 'Love your neighbor as yourself'" (Matthew 22:37–39).

But when Jesus spoke to the disciples, He had even more specific instructions about what it looks like to put God first. I think that's important because, when you make a decision to follow God, there needs to be more of Him and less of you. Jesus was explicit about this to His disciples as they were preparing to go out and begin spreading the gospel for the first time.

In Matthew 10, Jesus told His followers to go after "the lost sheep of Israel" and to rely on God for provisions on their journey, not taking money or even a bag with them. He then told the disciples, "Whoever does not take up their cross and follow me is not worthy of me. Whoever finds their life will lose it, and whoever loses their life for my sake will find it" (Matthew 10:38–39).

The idea of literally losing your life for God is something the disciples didn't really understand at the time. They had given up their jobs and homes to follow Jesus. But Jesus was telling them that, sometimes, the sacrifice He calls us to is even more real.

In the Gospel of John, Jesus prepared His disciples for the trials ahead, both literal and figurative. Jesus explained to them what would happen to Him in ways the disciples hadn't yet comprehended. And to help them understand, He told them, "My command is this: Love each other as I have loved you. Greater love has no one than this: to lay down one's life for one's friends" (John 15:12–13).

Jesus's followers would eventually live this out in both inspiring and harrowing ways. Almost all of them would die in ways, like Jesus, that were both physically excruciating and politically significant. James the Lesser was stoned and beaten to death according to Jewish historians. Andrew was crucified on an X-shaped cross. Peter was crucified upside down at his request, because he said he felt unworthy to die in the same manner as his Lord. Paul was famously persecuted and beheaded by the Roman emperor Nero.

I'm obviously still alive, so I haven't actually lost my life in the physical sense for Him just yet. I am still, thanks to God's grace, in the process of dying to myself figuratively so that, when people look at me, they see more of Him.

But I can understand and relate to the call Jesus had for His followers and the ultimate sacrifice some of them made. Because, while not for reasons of religious persecution, in the process of doing the thing I felt God called me to do, I very nearly died.

On November 4, 1988, all our hard work finally came to fruition and opening night had arrived. The first game of the Hornets' first season had been an amazing success. Well, an amazing success considering we lost the game by almost forty points. We were hosting the Cleveland Cavaliers, a good team that was consistently in the playoffs. One of their best players was a seven-foot center named Brad Daugherty who had played at the University of North Carolina. But that night, the thing I was most impressed by was our fans. They didn't show up to see the other team. They showed up to support *our* team.

The entire night was *the* event in Charlotte.

Rick Hendrick still compares walking into our arena that night with the first time he ever walked into pit row for the Daytona 500. I imagine it must have been like how Noah felt when he first walked onto the ark with all the animals inside. He had been working toward this crazy dream, and here it was, fully realized.

I had just assumed it was customary that every game would begin with a prayer. And so, on the cusp of our first game ever, I had arranged for a local pastor to deliver the invocation.

Well, apparently that wasn't exactly how things were done in the NBA. Commissioner Stern called and told me I wasn't allowed to have a pregame prayer in the arena.

"David, I respect that you're the commissioner, and I know it's your league," I told him, "but I only have this team because of God. And the last thing I'm going to do is go back on my word to Him."

"George," he replied, "it's just not something you can do. There isn't a discussion to be had."

"David, I love you," I responded. And I meant it. "But I will fight you on this. And I'm in the Bible Belt. Who do you think is going to win?"

David understood, and I think he truly wanted our fans to be able to acknowledge God before games. We came to an agreement where we would have our prayers but just not broadcast them on national television.

Unlike Noah, we didn't have animals—unless you count the Hornet mascot. But we were still incredibly packed inside. We had a sellout crowd, and our fans came literally dressed to the nines. Some men wore tuxedos, and more than a few women put on their finest ball gowns. For the average NBA game, it was over the top. But as someone who had always appreciated formal attire, I have to say I was impressed. Still, while some of the crowd dressed nice, they knew why they were at the game. There was nothing formal about their enthusiasm for what was happening on the court. They cheered the entire game, and at the end, as the players walked off the court, our fans rose and gave them a standing ovation.

It was an incredible and surreal scene. Some of our players thought the crowd was cheering for the other team. "Why would they be cheering for us? We just lost by forty," they said.

However, after all the Cavaliers had left the court and only the Charlotte Hornets remained, our fans kept applauding. They didn't care about the score. They were just happy to have a team of their own to cheer for.

It was my first game as an owner, so I was obviously really excited as well. The result on the court could have been better, but I couldn't have been happier with the score in the stands. I had a few of our sponsors and biggest supporters with me, and I wanted to take them down to the locker room to meet the team. Well, when I walked in to tell our players how proud I was of them and make some introductions, I learned something else about the NBA. Apparently, coming into the locker room after the game, even as an owner, was a rookie mistake. At least after a game in which we lost by forty.

Kurt Rambis, one of the veterans we signed in the offseason who had won championships with the Los Angeles Lakers, asked me to take my guests and wait outside until the team had a chance to process the loss.

"This is our job," he explained to me. "We didn't do anything worthy of having people come in today. We'll meet you outside."

From my perspective, the night had been a smashing success. But I respected the standard the players wanted to hold themselves to. It's never fun to lose by forty, especially in your home debut. But I liked a lot of what I saw and was confident things would improve.

Meanwhile, I had to protect the name of our home court.

Before our first game, there was a push to change the name of the Charlotte Coliseum. The day of our next home game, there was a big meeting, with media and public officials. A lot of the entrenched powers that be—some local government officials and the "blue bloods" of Charlotte—wanted to change the name of the Coliseum to include a corporate sponsorship. I did not want to change the name. I wanted to keep it the Charlotte Coliseum. We were just on the verge of introducing our city to the country. The rest of the country didn't know if Charlotte was in North Carolina, South Carolina, Virginia, or even West Virginia.

At that meeting, while I was speaking, my left arm jerked several times, kind of uncontrolled. At first, I wondered if it was a case of nerves popping back up, like the first time I had addressed the Charlotte city council about my ideas for bringing the Hornets to town. I didn't have a clue what was going on. When I left to go to my car in the parking lot, even though it was early November, I was sweating profusely. I felt like I was going to faint. Thank God I didn't.

I lay down for a minute in my car, and once I felt better, I got up and went to the office. My team president, Spencer Stolpen, saw me when I walked in.

"George, you don't look good," he said.

I didn't feel good either, which confused me. It felt like I was weak, like I was hurt—but I couldn't understand why.

I figured I was coming down with something if Spencer was noticing. "Well, I wouldn't have come back here if you're going to tell me I don't look good," I said.

"No, you look pale, you look sick," he continued. "What's the matter?"

I didn't think anything was wrong. More importantly, I didn't have time for anything to be wrong. My basketball team was 0-2, having just lost a road game to the defending NBA champion, Detroit Pistons. More importantly, I was trying to keep our arena named after the city we were trying to represent. Plus, I had the day-to-day operations of George Shinn and Associates to look after. I was busy.

Too busy.

But Spencer was right. Something was wrong. I lay down on the couch and fell asleep. That's the last thing I remember. I don't know how I got from my office to the hospital. I don't remember going to the hospital. All I know is, I woke up, and there were nurses in my room. "Good morning, Mr. Shinn," they said. "We're glad you're okay. You've had a stroke."

At first, I was shocked. I couldn't imagine that something like this could happen to me. I had always prided myself in being in excellent shape. I ran five miles a day. I watched my diet. I didn't indulge in excessive drinking and never did drugs.

How could I have a stroke?

I learned later that I'd had the exact kind of stroke that killed my father when he was fifty. I was forty-eight.

The doctors told me my right frontal lobe had started bleeding in my brain. Had it happened anywhere else, they said, literally an inch on either side of where it happened, I would have been paralyzed.

I wasn't paralyzed. But they wouldn't let me leave the hospital for two weeks.

It's crazy to think about how God's hand could be in something that hospitalized me for fifteen days, but that's what happened. And let me tell you, that was an adjustment.

There's no question that I was a workaholic. I used to tell my team at George Shinn and Associates, "I only expect you to work half a day." They would smile and look up with some anticipation of being able to go home early. But then I told them what I meant. "And I don't care if it's the first twelve hours of the day or the second."

The thing is, I was working that hard, putting in those kind of hours, myself. My mother taught me to believe in God and work your tail off. I was really doing both, and I credited my success to that approach.

But believing in God also means believing in Him to provide as opposed to relying on yourself. The reason Jesus sent His disciples into towns and told them to take no money, or bags, or any of their own provisions was because He wanted to teach them to rely on God to provide. God provided the ram for Abraham in the bush. God provided the raven in the desert for Elijah. And God spiritually provided for the apostles as they began their own ministries.

God had provided for me too. But when you have success, it's easy to think your work is the reason for it, as opposed to God's grace. That being the case, I see God's hand in allowing my stroke to happen in a specific part of my brain that didn't paralyze me. I could have died from that stroke. As I lay there in the hospital, I realized I needed to figuratively die to myself as well.

I had never gone two days in a row in my adult life without going to work. The stroke made me go more than two weeks without doing anything.

And that's when God showed up.

I hate to admit it now, but as I prepared to return to work, I secretly hoped everything would be in disarray when I got back. I needed to be needed. I wanted to know that the amount of time and effort I had been putting in mattered. I don't think I realized it at the time, but I was holding on so tightly to my life, trying to be in control, that I didn't appreciate the amazing team God had put around me.

When I got back to the office, everything was just where I left it.

Well, except for one thing.

We had our second home game the night I had my stroke. While I was unconscious at the hospital, my team was taking on the Los Angeles Clippers, who at that time weren't one of the better teams in the league. Kurt Rambis, the veteran player who had asked us to wait outside the locker room after our first game, had seventeen points and fourteen rebounds. We beat the Clippers by twelve.

I wasn't there, of course, but the players, Coach Harter, and the assistants all decided to give the game ball—the ball from our first win as a franchise—to me. They all signed it, and it was placed on my desk, waiting for me when I returned to the office.

I've still got that basketball. It remains one of my most treasured possessions. I like to joke that I almost died to get our first win. I mean, it was like a movie script. But who would write something as crazy as everything that happened?

Only God. But He didn't just write it for our amusement. He writes our stories for our sanctification.

Having survived the stroke, I was more excited than ever to still be a part of God's story. I knew our team was a part of it too. So, even though I knew I couldn't go to the games in the way I had gone to the first one, doing all the networking and talking and connecting, I still wanted to be there.

I mean, we weren't in first place, but the other expansion team that started the same season as us, the Miami Heat, had lost their first thirteen games. We had already won four times!

I had to figure out how to go to the games in a way that wouldn't draw attention to myself or away from the team.

Spencer Stolpen, the man who had driven me to the hospital, took me to the arena twice in a covert operation we jokingly referred to as "Mission Impossible."

He would drop me off in a special reserved parking lot and then ushers would let me in through a side exit that was normally locked. From there, they slowly walked me to my seats just before the opening tip.

Being in the arena, looking out over the sea of people who had gathered together not just to see a basketball game but—at least in my eye—to celebrate God's good work, was incredibly restorative. The people in the stands were so supportive not just of the team but of me. I got more than one thousand cards and letters saying they were praying for me and hoping I would get better soon.

I did—thanks to the people of Charlotte and their prayers.

The Bible is clear about the power of prayer.

It's also very clear about the necessity of rest.

If you went to Sunday school, you probably learned the Ten Commandments. Some of them are easy enough to rattle off:

Thou shall not put any gods before Me.

Thou shall not murder.

Thou shall not commit adultery.

Thou shall not steal.

But sometimes we overlook, forget about, or simply downright ignore the fourth commandment: remember the Sabbath day and keep it holy.

To an Old Testament audience, that meant not just remembering God but not doing any work at all. I struggled with that concept earlier in my life, and it's something many of us struggle with today. In fact, we struggle with rest, biblically speaking, or observing the Sabbath. We sometimes go out of our way to brag about how hard we work.

I firmly believe God calls us to hard work and rewards us for it. But the temptation can easily become focused on the fruits we receive from the work *we've* done instead of the blessings God has provided for us. That's one reason I think He calls us to rest. We need to give ourselves a break, a chance to take our focus off anything we have gotten for ourselves and instead celebrate all God has given us.

If you think about it, it's really no different from when Jesus told His disciples to die to themselves and to love God with all their soul.

God wants us to make our lives about Him, not us. Not because He needs the attention or acclaim but because He is the source of all things good, including love. When we make our lives about anything else, we are cheapening our experience, and God wants only the best for us.

That's why it's easy for me to look back and see His hand throughout my entire life, even the hard parts.

Especially the hard parts.

I almost died the same day the NBA team I owned won its first game. I think God was trying to tell me something.

Looking back, I wish I would have been a better listener. A painful pattern in my life began to emerge. For the rest of my time as an NBA owner, when the team found success, sometimes along with it came some of my biggest personal failures.

CHAPTER 14

Building a Winning Team— On *and* Off the Court

Having survived—literally—my first win as an NBA owner, I tried to go about the business of running the team, keeping in mind the role God had played in not only *getting* me this far but *keeping* me there. I had worked hard to make the Hornets franchise into a reality. When I had the stroke, I really tried to see it as God reminding me that He was still CEO and that my job was to just listen to Him.

When David became king, and after "the Lord had given him rest" (2 Samuel 7:1), he prayed about what to do to honor the Lord. He asked the prophet Nathan if he should build a more permanent place for the people of God and His ark. David also asked what else he should do to please God.

Through Nathan, the Lord responded to David with some incredibly powerful and reassuring words. God reminded David who really was (and still is) in charge:

> "I took you from the pasture, from tending the flock,
> and appointed you ruler over my people Israel. I have
> been with you wherever you have gone, and I have cut

off all your enemies from before you. Now I will make your name great, like the names of the greatest men on earth. And I will provide a place for my people Israel and will plant them so that they can have a home of their own and no longer be disturbed." (2 Samuel 7:8–10)

I could relate to how David felt. You make it to the top, and then you feel like it's up to you to stay there. But the reality is, David didn't get to be king because of anything he did. In fact, we know from the Bible that God chose and blessed David without any action on his part. God's blessing allowed David to slay Goliath and ultimately become king.

That's the point that God, through the prophet Nathan, was making to David. God didn't need David to do anything for Him. David eventually understood this and responded to God by asking Him to "bless the house of your servant, that it may continue forever in your sight; for you, Sovereign Lord, have spoken, and with your blessing the house of your servant will be blessed forever" (2 Samuel 7:29).

And God did continue to bless David.

David enjoyed numerous military victories over much larger empires, and he expanded the reach of the kingdom of Israel as a result. More importantly, the people of Israel were blessed by David's righteousness and wisdom. That's the key takeaway: God blessed David so he could bless others.

I wasn't the king of Israel. But I tried to run my kingdom, which happened to be a basketball team, in such a way that it would be a blessing to the people in our community.

I'm happy to say, for a good stretch of time, we were a blessing to the city of Charlotte.

We were the smallest market in the NBA in terms of population, but our footprint kept growing well beyond the edge of town. The Chicago Bulls, including Michael Jordan, who had played at the University of North Carolina, came to our arena on December 23, 1988, that first season. The game was nationally televised, and we put on a show for the whole country, many of whom were seeing our team for the first time.

Michael Jordan scored thirty-three points, but Kurt Rambis tipped in the ball with .04 seconds left, and we won by two. When Kurt scored, I don't think I've ever heard a group of people make more noise in my life. The win over the Bulls was our introduction to the basketball world and the beginning of what came to be known as "Hornets Hysteria."

It was great for our fans to see Michael Jordan in person, but they were rooting for the Hornets—not that seeing some of the other world-class basketball players up close wasn't fun. We had a tradition of interviewing the "star of the game" on the court after the final buzzer. If we won, we interviewed a Hornets player. If we lost, we'd talk to one of the opposing players.

When Magic Johnson and the Lakers came to town, we asked him to be the "star of the game." Thousands of our fans were waiting in the arena to hear this NBA icon address them. While he was sitting on the chairs, before the interview began, our PR whiz Harold Kaufman threw him a Hornets T-shirt. The crowd started to chant for him to put it on. Magic looked up with that trademark grin and put on the Hornets shirt. The place went wild!

We had lost most of our games, usually by a ton of points, but our fans were having fun. We sold out every game that season. In fact, we would sell out our first three hundred and sixty-four games, leading the league in attendance for years. Considering we were the smallest city in the league, I couldn't help but see God in that.

In fact, I think God helped our attendance in even more direct ways.

Despite David Stern's opposition, I continued our tradition of having someone pray before every home game. I'd often invite a pastor from a nearby church to do it. When the pastor of a church got the chance to pray over twenty-four thousand people, a lot of his congregants showed up. Often, many of those congregants would end up buying season tickets. I have no doubt that inviting God into our business made our business better in every way.

The people of Charlotte were in love with their Hornets, and the team was in love with the city. If a player scored forty points, he did the weather on the local TV station. Guard Kelly Tripucka did it several times. Our players were regularly stopped on the street or at restaurants and asked for autographs. Even I got to enjoy a few perks.

One time when I was going to the office, traffic was so backed up that it was causing me to be late for a meeting. I pride myself on punctuality, so I looked for a way to get around the traffic and make it to my office in time. To do that, I turned down a street I wasn't supposed to, drawing the attention of a nearby police officer. The officer flashed his lights, pulled me over, and walked up to my window.

"Good afternoon, officer," I said cheerily. I was annoyed that I would be even later for the meeting and about the money I would have to pay for the ticket. I might have owned an NBA franchise, but I never liked to waste money.

"Just stay right there," the officer said somewhat gruffly, taking my driver's license and registration with him back to his car.

After a few moments, he returned to my window and handed me my identification and registration back.

"Mr. Shinn, I'm not giving you a ticket," he said, to my surprise. "But I thought it was important for you to stay here; otherwise people would have been complaining about it. I wanted them to think I was giving you the rundown, because they knew who you were too."

The city was with me and our team.

We won twenty games that first season, and we lost sixty-two. Instead of being disappointed that we didn't do better in the standings, our fans wanted to celebrate the fact we had completed our first season. The city threw us a parade, and thousands of fans lined the streets of downtown Charlotte. We had players sit in Corvettes, Mustangs, and on top of open-air convertibles. Some of the older players were a little embarrassed by all the hoopla at first, especially after a losing season. But when they saw the enthusiasm of the fans and the support they had for our team, they got into it. It was just our first season. We knew we were headed for bigger things, including a better record.

We still lost a lot over the next few seasons though. In fact, we won only nineteen games, one less than the year before, in the 1989–90 season. But because we lost, we got a high draft pick, which we used to select Kendall Gill, a small forward from Illinois who would become a key player for us.

The year after that, while our team still lost more games than we won, our franchise and city hit the big time. Partly because of our tremendous fan support, Charlotte was selected to host the 1991 All-Star Game.

"Many years ago, when Charlotte first applied for an NBA franchise, the joke among some of the media was, 'Where's Charlotte?'" David Stern said at his press conference the Saturday before the game. "I think this franchise and this city have answered that question in record-breaking fashion. The reception we've received our All-Star weekend from the people down here proves that this is a great basketball state."

The entire weekend was an incredible success. Two of our players, Rex Chapman and Kendall Gill, competed in the Slam Dunk Contest, which was won by Boston Celtic Dee Brown with a dunk while he was covering his eyes. The game on Sunday saw the best basketball players on the planet playing against each other, right there in downtown Charlotte.

One columnist for the *Charlotte Observer*, Ron Green, wrote after the game:

> Fifty years ago, Charlotte was Mayberry. . . . Five years ago, George Shinn, a little fellow with a sunshine smile and an absurd idea, was telling us he would get us an NBA franchise and we were saying, well, yeah, OK George. Someone out west wrote that the only franchise Charlotte would get would be one with golden arches. But we got it. And today, the NBA All-Star Game is being played in Mayberry. Because of Shinn, who started all of this.

It really was a sight to behold.

I have to admit that I let some of it go to my head.

We were in Boone, North Carolina, at the beginning of one season for our team's training camp, which we held at Appalachian State University. I had taken our family to Wendy's for dinner. After we finished ordering, the manager came up to me with a pen and paper in his hand.

"Mr. Shinn, would you mind signing this for me?" he said with a smile on his face.

"Sure," I said, grabbing the pen. I'd signed plenty of autographs before. I'd even learned of a way to sign them that I thought was really clever. The Los Angeles Dodgers had won baseball's World Series in 1988, and their manager, the always colorful Tommy Lasorda, had become somewhat of a friend of mine. He signed a picture for me that said, "You and the Dodgers are great."

I liked that positive message. So, I started signing something similar. I took the paper from the Wendy's manager and signed my name, along with, "You and the Hornets are great."

I was about to hand it back to him when I took a better look at what I had signed. It was just the receipt for our meal.

Off the court, I thought our team was a tremendous success. On the court, eventually, as losing seasons turned into high draft picks and good players, our team became successful too.

In 1991, we won the draft lottery and got the number one overall pick of all the players in college basketball. We took a forward from UNLV named Larry Johnson, who had won a national championship in college under famous coach Jerry Tarkanian. Larry had a terrific season and won Rookie of the Year for the entire league.

The next year, we missed the playoffs again but won the second overall pick in the draft. I was disappointed to miss out on Shaquille O'Neal, who went first to the Orlando Magic, but getting Alonzo Mourning, a center from Georgetown, with the second pick was a nice consolation prize. Alonzo's size, talent, and competitive drive proved to be the final ingredients we needed to become a legitimate playoff team.

With a new coach in Allan Bristow and a starting five of Muggsy Bogues, Dell Curry, Kendall Gill, Larry Johnson, and Alonzo Mourning, we had our first-ever winning season and made the playoffs, where we faced the legendary Boston Celtics in the first round.

I can't tell you how gratifying it was, two years after we hosted the All-Star Game, to be able to bring playoff basketball to Charlotte. Playing our first-ever playoff game against such an iconic franchise like Boston made it all the more meaningful.

I still remembered when Celtics owner and Hall of Fame coach Red Auerbach had embraced me after my speech at the board of governors' meeting when I was trying to win a franchise. Now I was trying to win a playoff series against his team.

Larry Bird had retired the previous season, but they still had warriors from their championship teams like Kevin McHale and Robert Parish.

The Celtics were part of the NBA's old guard. We were the new wave, eager to see how we stacked up. The first round back then was best three out of five.

We lost our first-ever playoff game in Boston but came back and won a thriller in game two in double overtime.

In our first-ever home playoff game, with our fans screaming and cheering the entire game, we beat Boston by thirty. Up two games to one, we now had a chance to win our very first playoff series—and we had a chance to do it in front of our home fans.

I can't tell you how hard I was praying.

I know God doesn't take sides in sporting events, so I'm not saying what happened next was an answer to my prayer. But I am saying what happened next was that the people of Charlotte and the entire basketball world saw one of the most iconic moments in our franchise history.

Down by one with twenty seconds to go, we gave the ball to Larry Johnson, who went one-on-one to try and win the game. He missed, but the ball went out of bounds off a Boston player with three seconds to go.

We had one more chance to win the game. Dell Curry inbounded from the baseline and found Alonzo Mourning wide open at the top of the key. He took one dribble to his right, rose, and shot the ball. The crowd rose in anticipation, and when the ball went through the net with no time remaining, Hornets Hysteria became national news. Our arena exploded, with everyone in their seats cheering, crying, hugging their neighbors, and losing their voices.

It was a sight to behold and truly one of the highlights of my life.

We would lose in the next round of the playoffs to the New York Knicks, but in terms of our place in the basketball world, we had arrived. And I was ready to do what it took to keep us there.

In that offseason, the accountants and general manager told me that, eventually, the players' rookie contracts would expire. We would need to sign our best players to bigger deals. So, as a sign of our commitment to keeping our team competitive, I signed Larry Johnson to the biggest contract in the history of professional sports.

For comparison's sake, at the time, Barry Bonds was the highest-paid baseball player, making $43 million over six years.

In hockey, Wayne Gretzky had recently signed a three-year extension worth $25.5 million. Steve Young was the NFL's highest-paid player, with a contract that paid him $26.75 million over five years.

We signed Larry Johnson to a twelve-year deal worth $84 million.

I wanted to demonstrate to the city that I was prepared to invest in keeping us on the national stage. I may not have been a blue blood, but I liked playing with the big boys.

I soon realized, though, that some of the other NBA boys were a lot bigger than me.

The following year, we approached Alonzo Mourning, who had one year left on his rookie contract, about signing an extension like Larry Johnson did.

Like Larry, Alonzo continued to excel for us. Although we didn't make it out of the first round of the playoffs, we had a good, talented, and young team that was exciting to watch.

I originally had offered Mourning, through his agent, David Falk, a ten-year contract worth $70 million. That was more than double what I had paid for the entire franchise less than a decade before. Falk, who represented Michael Jordan, among others, said my offer didn't come close to what his client was looking for.

It was an incredibly difficult situation. Since I had already committed so much to Larry, there were limits to what I felt I could reasonably do.

David Falk told me my offer wouldn't get it done. I increased it to over $11 million a year, keeping in mind the financial restraints we were under, especially considering our arena didn't have the skyboxes other cities had that brought in the big money.

It wasn't enough for Alonzo and his agent.

"No," they told me. "You've got to get closer to my money."

It just broke my heart.

Since they told me in no uncertain terms that Alonzo wouldn't be signing a new contract at the end of the upcoming season, I made the difficult decision to authorize a trade. In November 1995, we traded Alonzo Mourning to the Miami Heat, getting back sharpshooting Glen Rice, among other players, in return.

Losing Alonzo was really tough, but I tried to stay open about it in terms of my trust with God. I hadn't done anything to deserve the fortune of getting players like Larry and Alonzo. God had blessed our town by blessing my team with them. And we had been blessed.

I hoped that, even without our best player, our team would still be one that excited our fans and would make a major contribution to the city of Charlotte.

Our team stayed competitive and won a lot of games. In fact, we actually got better because of how good of a player Glen Rice turned out to be. He would actually win the 1997 NBA All-Star Game MVP award, getting his picture—and the name *Charlotte* on the front of his jersey—in papers all over the country.

My focus would soon turn away from the things happening on the court. I was openhanded in terms of inviting God into my professional life and trusting Him there; but I had started to grab things for myself in my personal life, things I knew I shouldn't have wanted. Those choices would lead to a much tougher battle, both with God and man, than anything my basketball team would ever face.

CHAPTER 15

Pride Cometh Before the Fall

In one of the greatest pieces of literature and theology ever written, the apostle Paul declared in the book of Romans, "And we know that in all things God works for the good of those who love him, who have been called according to his purpose" (Romans 8:28).

I absolutely believe Paul's word are true. My goal in life has been to serve God. I haven't always done it perfectly, and at times I've failed spectacularly. But if you take anything from my story, I want it to be that no matter how much we mess up, we can never outrun God's desire to use us according to His will. The Bible tells us God is love. And He forgives. It's up to us to look past our own faults and set our eyes on His perfection.

If you can do that, you can actually see what Paul meant in Romans 8:28. God uses *all* things for our benefit and for His glory. Basically, Paul's words mean that God uses the bumps in our roads to set us straight.

And I've traveled along a road with some serious bumps.

I have to admit that, as the Hornets became more successful, I found myself wavering and wandering from God. This happened in a few different areas, but the most significant one was in my marriage.

I had been married to Carolyn for nearly twenty-five years. We raised a family together and were blessed with three wonderful children. We tried to be good stewards of God's other blessings in our lives by starting a charitable foundation together, which donated to life-changing work in the Charlotte area.

However, I must admit to not always being the best husband.

Some people think marriage needs to be a 50/50 proposition. Well, having been married three times now, I can tell you that's just not true. If marriage is 50/50, then everyone is always keeping score and worried about whose turn it is to give and to get.

A good marriage needs to be 100/100, where each person is giving 100 percent of themselves for the other person.

As the Hornets had more success, and as my profile grew higher in the Charlotte area and around the country, I stopped giving 100 percent to my marriage. Carolyn's and my interests started to grow further apart. As a result, so did we.

Unfortunately, those are the kind of spaces that leave men vulnerable to bad decisions. I was no different.

Because I was in the news quite often, women would sometimes see me and recognize me as someone who was very successful. That kind of affirmation and validation can be just as alluring as the actual attention from the women. The more Carolyn and I grew apart, the more time I was by myself until, eventually, I let my eyes wander. And once your eyes start to wander, it's hard to train them back on God.

This is a problem the Bible talks about in very explicit ways. After he slayed Goliath, David would eventually become the king of Israel. As king, David had many great victories and was, as the Bible tells us, a man after God's own heart. But his eyes were also prone to wandering.

As recounted in 2 Samuel, King David was walking on his rooftop and saw a beautiful woman, Bathsheba, bathing. David was so struck by her beauty that he had a moment of weakness.

We all have moments of weakness, and that weakness inevitably leads to sin, even if it's just impure thoughts. That's why we need God's grace.

But David didn't just have impure thoughts. He continued to sin. He made arrangements to see Bathsheba, even after finding out she was married and that her husband was in David's army. David summoned Bathsheba to his palace, where, the Bible tells us, they slept together.

I know what that's like.

I had begun to let my eyes wander. Eventually, I started to arrange to see some of the people my eyes found. It was a season in my life I'm not proud of, but it is a part of the road that has led me to where I am today. I allowed myself to travel down roads and to places I had no business being. But God, in His loving way, let me go there because I still had a lot to learn about following God and surrendering "me."

In the fall of 1997, in this season of wandering, I was visiting a nephew who was living in a treatment facility down in South Carolina. After talking with him and trying to offer words of encouragement, I headed back to my car in the parking lot. I got in my driver's seat and started the engine, and when I put the car into gear I looked up and slammed on the brakes. Standing in front of me was a woman I'd never seen before. She had basically positioned herself to block my car, so I couldn't drive away.

"What are you doing?" I demanded. "I need to leave."

She walked over to my passenger side and opened the door and sat down in the car next to me. I was so shocked that I was momentarily speechless. What was happening?

"I'd like to talk to you. Can we go somewhere to have lunch?" she said.

"I'm not going to lunch," I said. I was so confused.

"Well, I need to talk to you," she said. "Can we get somewhere more private?"

She explained that she was getting a divorce and wanted some advice about a lawyer.

I did have to go, but there was obviously something in me that liked the idea of seeing her.

Looking back, this was obviously a massive mistake. But when you start letting voices other than God's into your head, you start to let other ideas take hold, and sin can sound sensible. I did have a place on the lake nearby. This woman was paying me attention and wanting me to pay attention to her.

And I had a hard time ignoring attention from others.

I took her to my lake house to talk. When we got there, she asked if she could see inside. I was proud of it, so I gave her a tour. Once we got to my bedroom, she became very . . . affectionate. We did not sleep together, but we certainly engaged in some inappropriate bedroom behavior.

Afterward, I brought her back to the facility where she, like my nephew, was receiving treatment for addiction. I went back home and continued on with my life. To be honest, I didn't think much of it. Then, one day, the weight of my sin came crashing down on me.

The woman and her husband tried to blackmail me, saying that they would accuse me of sexual assault unless I paid them off. I was mortified because of their false accusation but also because, while these people were clearly in the wrong, so was I.

My lawyers told me my life would be a lot easier if I just paid them money to go away.

I knew they were right, but something inside me just wouldn't go along with it. Even if I paid the woman and her husband, what assurances did I have that they would actually go away?

Besides that, I already had to endure the more embarrassing and difficult time of admitting my failures to my wife. I'd hurt her and our marriage in a way that would change and harm many lives.

Paying off my accuser wouldn't save my marriage. So I told them I wasn't going to give them any money. The next thing I knew, she had filed sexual assault charges against me, and I was being interrogated by a South Carolina State Law Enforcement detective. Prosecutors opened an investigation and ultimately decided not to file any criminal charges.

To be honest, I was never really worried about that, because I knew I was innocent. But then I was told the woman filed a civil suit against me for emotional damages. That meant there would be a trial.

Of course, because of my high profile, the media was interested. Court TV decided to broadcast the entire thing to the whole country.

I think there's an incredibly important spiritual lesson here. Part of how I rationalized my behavior was based on my incredible success. With that success came fame and popularity.

And, I admit, I reveled in all of it. I rarely turned down an interview, and I liked being known as a successful man. When you come from where I came from, it's hard not to take pride in being where I was.

But Proverbs 16:18 says it best: "Pride goes before destruction, a haughty spirit before a fall."

I had clearly been prideful. Now I was definitely falling.

I was praying quite a bit in the lead-up to the trial. It's amazing how often we do that, right? We rely on God in times of hardship, and as soon as things become comfortable, we look away. Well, I was back in a season of hardship and was praying more than ever. In that season of prayer, I heard God tell me that the most dangerous thing in my life right now, as a result of my sin, was stress.

I knew I was in for a lot of stress. A nationally televised trial exposing all my sins and failures is literally one of the most stressful things I could imagine. So, in praying to God about it, I felt like He was telling me to seek medical help.

I called my doctor and asked that he check me out thoroughly to make sure I was physically well. I'd heard about people getting cancer and dying during incredibly difficult times.

Basically, I wanted to make sure the stress I was about to endure wouldn't kill me.

His response after my checkup didn't exactly make things better.

After a round of X-rays and a battery of tests, my doctor said, "I'll call you later to let you know."

The call finally came the next morning.

"I didn't tell you last night because I didn't want you to lose any sleep," my doctor said. "But you've got a spot on your lung in one of the pictures. It looks like it could be cancer."

I started praying immediately.

"I want you to come back later today, if possible," he said, somewhat cautiously. "I want you to do some new tests because the pictures can occasionally make something that isn't bad look worse than it actually is. So, don't get too worried just yet."

Even at my current age, many memories still come to my mind clear as day. Hanging up the phone with my doctor that day and dropping onto my knees immediately after is one of them.

"Please God, help me," I pleaded. "Please be with me. I know I've messed up, but I can't get through this on my own."

The next day, I went back into the hospital to do new tests. This time the doctor stayed with me as the tests were run.

After a few moments, he looked up at me and smiled.

"You're good," he said. "It was a bad photo."

In that moment, I knew God had done this. I also knew in that moment that, despite everything I'd done, I was going to be alright. That was the thing that carried me through the entire trial.

Every step of the way, as hard as it was to walk through, I felt like God was by my side.

"Lord, I hate going through this," I said often. "But just help me get through it."

The trial was in Columbia, South Carolina. After initially trying to stay in the area, the attention from reporters, who called my hotel room at all hours of the night, proved to be too much. It was already a turbulent time for my soul. The phone calls at all hours gave me too many restless nights. I literally couldn't get any sleep.

I eventually decided to just stay in Charlotte and fly down every day for the trial.

My lawyers wanted me to testify and thought putting me on first might catch their lawyers off guard. Plus, they thought if I testified and told the truth first, it would set the tone for the entire trial. And so, on national television, I had to talk about the nature of my extramarital affairs and the nature of my interaction with this woman specifically.

But as embarrassing as it was, the verdict was ultimately fair. My attorney, Bill Diehl, was able to demonstrate that her claims were not only false but also physically impossible.

Though I felt humiliated, I knew the outcome would be good only because of God.

After closing remarks, the jury left to deliberate.

For whatever reason, I didn't want to be there anymore. I had gone through the trial and endured the tribulations and humiliation in the face of the world. *These are the people you wanted to please,* I felt God was saying. *Now learn that the only one whose love you need is Mine.*

With that peace of mind, I asked Bill if I actually needed to be there as the jury deliberated. "Can I go?" I asked him. "My plane is here. I'd like to just fly back."

It was a civil trial, so I would not be facing arrest if a bad verdict came back.

"If you want to go, go," Bill told me.

So, I got up and left. I flew back by myself. It was a strange moment, having just endured an experience like that and now looking out the window of a plane, reflecting on the lessons God wanted me to learn from it.

Ultimately, my own sin was the reason I had to deal with those consequences. When Joseph was tempted in the Bible, he resisted I didn't. And when you welcome temptation, there are consequences to pay.

I deserved what I got. But with God, I also got more than I deserved.

My plane landed, and I got into my car and began the drive back to my home. My wife Carolyn, understandably, had filed for divorce by then, so I was literally alone, driving along the highway, looking for something to listen to on the radio. Once again, my search for music was stopped by hearing voices on the radio. This time it wasn't Dr. Peale. It was the news, and they were talking about me.

"The jury has reached a verdict in the George Shinn trial," the announcers said. "We will go now live to the courtroom."

I pulled over and started praying. It was a little different from the first time I had prayed to God on the side of the road. Then I was at the end of my rope, with no hopes other than to turn to God and invite Him into my life as my business partner and CEO. He had been incredibly faithful, and I can look back and see that all the success I had in the three decades since then was because of Him.

Sadly, I didn't always remember that along the way.

I had forgotten too many times, and I had started to think I deserved the credit for my successes and acclaim. As humiliating as this trial had been, I was still grateful for it, because I knew God was using it to bring me back into His presence. That's where I was now—once again pleading with God on the side of the road, this time listening to the radio as a jury decided whether I'd been telling the truth.

I heard the judge say, "Before we hear from the jury, I want to remind everyone in attendance about the proper decorum. I won't have any outbursts in my courtroom.

"If you do," he continued, "I'll have you taken out."

At least I knew I wouldn't be in trouble with the judge.

I started to hear the voice of a juror, though making out what they were saying was challenging. It wasn't hard to know the outcome though.

All of a sudden, I heard a loud scream come from my speakers, and I knew immediately it was my lawyer, Bill. I never even heard the words, "We find for the defendant." I didn't need to. Bill's scream told me everything I needed to hear.

I started crying again, and just started praising God, thanking Him not just for protecting me and helping me get through this ordeal but also for loving me in spite of my disobedience.

Sitting in my car, I was reminded of something my father told me before he passed away. I was seven, and we were out walking in the woods near our property and had come to a creek.

"Would it be okay to get a drink from the creek?" I remember asking him.

"Of course, Junior," he replied.

I walked over and bent down, cupping my hands and preparing to dip them in the cool rushing water. Just before I did, though, I looked up and saw a giant pile of manure in the water near me.

"Dad," I said as I stood up. "I can't drink this water. Look at this." That's when he told me something I've never forgotten.

"Son, in your life, you're going to walk into a lot of messes," he said.

"But you know, if you have the courage to walk past it, either upstream or down, you'll find that what seems like impossible messes don't actually amount to all that much," my dad added.

He was right. With God's help, I had walked past the mess. And now it didn't seem like all that much.

My phone dinged, telling me I had a text. I looked at it. David Stern, the commissioner of the NBA, had messaged me one word.

"Yahoo."

I appreciated the support, but I knew I had a lot of work to do.

In the Bible, David was confronted about his sin by the prophet Nathan, who delivered a message from the Lord:

> Out of your own household I am going to bring calamity on you. Before your very eyes I will take your wives and give them to one who is close to you, and he will sleep with your wives in broad daylight. You did it in secret, but I will do this thing in broad daylight before all Israel. (2 Samuel 12:11–12)

David was terrified, but Nathan offered him reassurance. "The LORD has taken away your sin. You are not going to die" (2 Samuel 12:13).

David repented immediately, but he still faced punishment. The child David conceived with Bathsheba became ill and died after seven days.

After being informed that his son had died, the Bible tells us, "David got up from the ground. After he had washed, put on lotions and changed his clothes, he went into the house of the LORD and worshiped" (2 Samuel 12:20).

David's actions were wrong. Not only did his first son with Bathsheba die but so did Bathsheba's first husband, Uriah, a soldier in David's army. To cover up his own sin, David ordered Uriah to be in the front of the battle, knowing he would be killed.

Like David, I was glad to have survived and grateful that the Lord had taken away my sin. But the story of my sin also involves the loss of life.

Shortly after the verdict, my accuser's husband—who had been part of the plan to extort money from me—took his own life. It was a tragedy all the way around, but our tragedies are the ingredients of God's triumphs. Through it all, I still felt the overwhelming sense of peace knowing that, in spite of my own failure, I was still a part of God's story.

I had sinned against the Lord. But I knew I was still in His will.

His forgiveness made engaging in public life so much easier. But I would still face consequences for my actions.

CHAPTER 16

Dust and Ashes

If you ever find yourself questioning God's sovereignty during our times of hardship and loss, I can't recommend the book of Job strongly enough.

Job was a righteous man who was "blameless and upright" in God's eyes (Job 1:1). But Satan, ever the tempter, suggested to God that Job's piety was only because of the blessings God had given him. After all, Job was wealthy and had been blessed with children and a wife.

God permitted Satan to take Job's possessions and even his children. However, God instructed Satan not to harm Job physically. After Job was informed that his land was gone and all ten of his children had died, he refused to turn from God. Even after Satan inflicted Job's body with boils and his wife suggested he curse God and die, Job simply asked, "Shall we receive good from God, and shall we not receive evil?" (Job 2:10 ESV).

Things only got worse for Job, and after several conversations with his friends, who suggested that a just God wouldn't permit a righteous man like him to suffer, Job called out and questioned God.

Then, God answered Job:

Do you have an arm like God's, and can your voice thunder like his? Then adorn yourself with glory and splendor, and clothe yourself in honor and majesty. Unleash the fury of your wrath, look at all who are proud and bring them low, look at all who are proud and humble them, crush the wicked where they stand. Bury them all in the dust together; shroud their faces in the grave. Then I myself will admit to you that your own right hand can save you. (Job 40:9–14)

I know I'm not Job. He was blameless. I certainly was not. But it was useful to lean on his story and see how he was led by God to ultimate surrender, though not without his own questions and challenges.

The hardest part about going through challenges is thinking that your own hands and your own works can save you. I definitely experienced that after the trial. Things only got harder. At times, difficult situations made me look for solutions with my own hands instead of God's.

Initially, while the trial had been embarrassing for me personally and for the people of Charlotte, who didn't appreciate the negative publicity, the NBA community was very understanding and forgiving. David Stern would regularly check on me and offered me sound counsel and friendship throughout the ordeal.

The trial was over, but I still carried the shame and guilt with me. I remember the first owners' meeting I attended. I was hesitant to go. The trial hadn't been that long ago and, to be honest, I was embarrassed. But David Stern told me, in no uncertain terms, to basically get over myself.

"I want you to come up here," he told me. "You're going to be fine. You need to get yourself out and about and get this behind you."

I flew to New York and walked into the meeting room, as I'd done before, with all the other owners. David called me up to the front where he was standing, put his arms around me, and started speaking to the other owners.

"George is one of our own," he said. "He was accused of something he didn't do. But he didn't hide. He didn't cover it up and take the easy way out. He stuck it out and went through hell as a result. But he's here now, and he needs our support."

All the owners in the room stood up and started applauding.

The rest of the NBA community was largely supportive as well.

That following February, the All-Star Game weekend was hosted by the Golden State Warriors in the Bay Area. I had largely stayed away from Hornets games, just because of what I perceived to be the general sentiment back home. The media coverage over my behavior had become toxic. I know I messed up, but now incredibly exaggerated rumors about me spread through town, and outright lies about my character were repeated among the fans and sometimes even reported in the media. I was told to stay out of the headlines and just keep my mouth shut. It was incredibly difficult.

There in the hopeful anonymity of California, though, and because of the welcoming nature of my fellow owners, I thought it was safe for me to go out in public.

I was walking around the arena when, all of a sudden, a guy in a Warriors T-shirt came up to me.

"Oh my! You're George Shinn!" he shouted.

I looked around sheepishly, not knowing what to expect, but preparing for the worst. "Well, yes, I am," I said.

"Oh wow. I followed your trial."

It was sad to realize I was now known for a different type of story. All the times I had spoken at churches or shared my faith and relationship with God were now forgotten, replaced by my testimony in court about my moral failures. Thankfully, I knew God was giving me the rest of my life to work on changing that.

However, the reputational damage I had suffered in the present time was very real.

I had some people tell me that I should call a press conference and ask forgiveness from the city of Charlotte.

For a few different reasons, that didn't appeal to me. Mostly, I felt like I had gotten on my knees and asked God for forgiveness. I knew He had forgiven me, and Scripture told me that His Son, Jesus, had erased my sins. If God had forgiven me, what else really mattered?

That might have been shortsighted, because people in North Carolina would show me less grace than God.

I did talk to my kids. I told them what I probably should have told the public.

"I messed up," I told them. "I hurt your mom. I hurt you. I hurt our family. I'm sorry."

My wife divorced me. Between the trial and some of the changes we made with the team, the people of Charlotte started to separate from me too.

We stayed competitive after trading Alonzo Mourning. However, the cost of doing business in the NBA was rising, and our revenues weren't. I began to learn that the term *facilities arms race* is used in sports for a reason.

Basically, the salary cap continued to rise in the NBA, meaning owners expected to spend more money on players each year. Some of that was offset by the national TV contracts that owners all split. But each market has some differences in terms of how they make money. Their arenas each generate a different amount depending on how many tickets they sell and how many luxury boxes they have. While a ticket might be twenty dollars, luxury box seats can go for thousands of dollars, so the more of them you have in an arena, the more money you make.

Some of the arenas in bigger markets had a lot of luxury boxes; we had very few. That discrepancy is one reason why a city like Miami could afford to sign Alonzo Mourning to a bigger contract than we could. Plus, the Heat were in a bigger TV market, so their local broadcast contract brought them more money.

Basically, the realities of operating in a smaller market were starting to impact us. When our attendance had been the best in the league, it helped us be competitive. But after we traded some of our better players—including Larry Johnson and Muggsy Bogues—it sapped our fans' enthusiasm and attendance dropped. Then the accusations about me and the subsequent public trial devastated the fans.

Our attendance went from being top in the league to dropping to the bottom third. It was like the people of Charlotte were staying away from the team as a way of rejecting me.

As a result, my finances started to take a big hit, and I decided to take on a partner.

Initially, I had conversations with Michael Jordan. He had retired from the Chicago Bulls a few seasons before and was looking for ways to become an owner. The idea of being in business with the greatest player in NBA history was obviously exciting, especially with his local ties, including playing at the University of North Carolina. Ultimately, he wanted more of a stake in the team than I was looking to sell.

When that didn't work out, I turned to an Atlanta businessman named Ray Wooldridge. I thought the infusion of his capital would help keep our team competitive, a necessity since we were asking the city of Charlotte to build and help fund a new downtown arena.

We proposed a whole entertainment and retail development right in the heart of Charlotte, with the arena as the central piece. The new home for the Hornets, partly because of me, got the most scrutiny in the press.

The whole project was going to cost $192 million, which we were going to pay the majority of. We were prepared to kick in $109 million, which we could have done by raising $59 million from the up-front sale of luxury suites and club seats, not to mention the revenue we would have made from concessions, naming rights, and other money makers. I was also going to pay for up to $10 million out of my own pocket.

After we borrowed $50 million as a team and downtown businesses chipped in $25 million, we asked the city to contribute $58 million for the arena. I thought it was a fair deal, since, like the Coliseum had been, this new arena would be owned by the city.

Partly because of general sentiment toward me, my new co-owner, Ray Wooldridge, was the point person when it came to working with the city to drum up support.

We needed public support because the NBA in general was becoming less popular. The 1999–2000 season started late due to a lockout, as the owners and players' union negotiated a new labor agreement. Understandably, fans were frustrated with both sides.

That frustration would soon give way to unadulterated shock and grief.

A few years earlier, in 1997, we had signed a guard in free agency named Bobby Phills. Bobby was a tough, hard-nosed wing who played all out every time, shooting well but also causing problems for opposing players. Michael Jordan had said Bobby was the best defender in the league. We signed him for seven years because we loved all the ingredients he brought to our backcourt and our team.

Bobby's energy and hustle had made him a fan favorite. One of his fans was my son Chris, who Bobby always made time to talk to.

That made what happened even more heartbreaking.

After our morning practice on January 12, 2000, Bobby and our starting point guard, David Wesley, were driving on a stretch of road less than a mile from the arena. Police would later determine that Bobby was traveling in his Porsche at over one hundred miles per hour. He lost control, spun out, and hit another car.

He died instantly.

Our whole team, along with the entire Charlotte community, was devastated. We postponed our game the following day and offered several players, including David Wesley, counseling.

Bobby's death was a tragedy that compounded some of the negativity surrounding the team. When we played the Cleveland Cavaliers, Bobby's old team, we retired his jersey, hanging his number 13 from the rafters.

It was an incredibly emotional moment, with people crying on the court and in the stands.

Our team found a way to play on. Bobby's jersey essentially served as a testament to our love for a player as well as the grief we still carried.

I'd never been through anything like that before. I talked to Rick Hendrick, who had been through a similar ordeal when his speedboat racer had died.

The counsel from a friend, and a chance to help others who were now suffering so much, helped take my mind off my own troubles and allowed me to focus on Bobby's wife, Kendall, and their two children, who were left to face a life without this incredible man.

I tried to move on from my scandals, but we had mounting evidence that our fans hadn't. Our attendance was cratering, putting even more strain on our finances and making a new arena even more of a necessity. Polls we conducted indicated that some of the fans were staying away because of me. The numbers were making staying in Charlotte impossible for me financially. We needed a new arena, and the city was going to conduct a nonbinding resolution to gauge public sentiment on the idea.

Leading up to the day of the vote, I was cautiously optimistic. I remembered the All-Star Game we hosted and the first playoff series we won—the men and women dressed up in tuxedos and ball gowns arriving for our first game in limousines, as well as the convertibles and Corvettes we rode in when the city threw us a parade after our first season, even though we won only twenty games.

I felt like God had been with us—and with *me*—since the beginning, and I knew He still was.

But the people of Charlotte weren't.

The nonbinding referendum failed, with 57 percent of voters rejecting the motion to help fund the new arena.

In hindsight, all those positive moments and memories of the Hornets were a long time ago. I realized my relationship with the people of Charlotte looked much like my relationship with my first wife. Over time, I became more distant. Now it seemed like they were saying they wanted a divorce. Only I would have to be the one to leave.

After the referendum, we began exploring alternate locations for the team. The Vancouver Grizzlies were also trying to relocate and had lined up Memphis as their preferred destination. We looked at Louisville, along with a possible partnership with Kentucky Fried Chicken. But the partnership would require us to change the name to the Kentucky Colonels and change our team colors to red to match Kentucky Fried Chicken. I wasn't going to do that.

We also looked at St. Louis, which was the biggest city actively recruiting a new team. In the end, though, New Orleans seemed to make the most sense. Ray Wooldridge, who had been urging us to move the team, had preliminary conversations with the city of New Orleans, corporate sponsors, and season ticket holders there before the referendum. New Orleans also had a brand-new arena, with many of the skybox suites we felt necessary to make the economics of running the team work.

In January 2002, we filed an application with the NBA's board of governors to officially relocate the team to New Orleans for the 2003 season.

Announcing our intention to leave Charlotte in the middle of a season was of course not ideal, and the team and fans took it as devastating news. I went from being unpopular to being public enemy number one.

Less than a decade earlier, I was the most popular guy in town. People even tried to convince me to run for governor. Now I was a pariah, and I wasn't sure if I could move with the team before getting run out of town.

In chapter 42 of the book of Job, after the Lord responded to his complaints, Job answered God:

> I know that you can do all things; no purpose of yours
> can be thwarted. . . . My ears had heard of you but now
> my eyes have seen you. Therefore I despise myself and
> repent in dust and ashes. (Job 42:2, 5–6)

That's basically how I left town.

I had lost many friends. Financially, we had hopes for better success but no guarantees. I was in bad shape now. The Lord hadn't taken everything from me as He had Job, but He had taken plenty.

And, unlike Job, who was blameless and upright, I had earned some of my consequences through my own sinful decisions. But if Job could cling to God when he hadn't done anything to deserve his afflictions, so could I when I was enduring only what I had brought on myself. No matter the reason, I've learned that in the hard times, the Lord wants us to cling to Him the most.

Heading to a new city, I was clinging to the Lord.

But I had no idea how much tighter my grip would have to get.

CHAPTER 17

A Fresh Start and Historic Tragedy

One thing I have learned definitively over the years is that, regardless of whatever is happening in your life, God has a plan. We may not always like it, but if we can stay focused on God and look for reasons to trust Him even in the hardest times, God will often bless us in what we perceive as chaos.

Many of us have heard about the miracle of Jesus walking on the water. It's a great lesson that, with Jesus, anything is possible. My favorite part of the story is when Peter, ever the enthusiastic disciple, stepped out of the boat and joined Jesus on the water.

As the Gospel of Matthew describes it, "Then Peter got down out of the boat, walked on the water and came toward Jesus. But when he saw the wind, he was afraid and, beginning to sink, cried out, 'Lord, save me!'" (Matthew 14:29–30).

The key to that entire passage is that Peter became afraid when he saw the wind. But why did Peter see the wind?

Because he took his eyes off Jesus. Peter was doing just fine as long as he was looking at Jesus. His first few steps out of the water were amazing! But when he turned his gaze from heavenly authority toward worldly circumstances, Peter became afraid and faltered, just like we, as broken humans, sometimes do.

Leaving my home state of North Carolina, especially leaving behind my friends and family from Charlotte, was tough. While New Orleans was embracing us with open arms, I knew the people who had helped make my NBA dream a reality had markedly different body language and feelings toward me now. Still, I tried not to focus on that. I trusted that moving to New Orleans was part of God's plan, and I asked Him to bless the move.

God's blessing is one of the most important things you can have in your life. Whether it's a business venture, a personal relationship, or an idea you feel God has planted in your mind, invite the Lord into that space and ask Him to partner with you in making it a reality. I've learned through my experience that if you don't proactively invite God into your life, He will use struggles and challenges you encounter to get your attention.

I thought I was doing an okay job of inviting God into my new chapter of life in New Orleans—but He gave me plenty of challenges along the way, just to make sure.

The first issue I had to deal with was some breaches of trust with my new co-owner, Ray Wooldridge. Actually, it reminds me a lot of what King David dealt with toward the end of his reign in Israel.

At the start of the book of 1 Kings, we read that David was "very old" and "he could not keep warm even when they put covers over him" (1 Kings 1:1). So, David was no longer ruling Israel with his full senses and faculties. Now, God had already told David that his son Solomon would be the next king of Israel and that He would bless his reign.

But David had other sons, and they had other ideas. Absent from his father's presence and attention, David's fourth son, Adonijah (who was born to his wife Haggith), declared himself king. The Bible tells us Adonijah had chariots and horses and fifty men run ahead of him and presented himself as king.

That's basically what Ray Wooldridge did. Because of the publicity issues related to my trial, I took a back seat both on the Charlotte referendum and subsequent negotiations with other cities we might relocate to. That meant Ray was front and center. Unfortunately, like Adonijah, he presented himself as having a little more authority than he actually did.

One of the issues was that, when securing agreements for season ticket sales, Ray misrepresented the number of sales he had acquired. The NBA wanted a guarantee for ticket sales for five years. Ray had signed up a large number of companies to commit to this, but then he had allowed the companies to sign a separate agreement, unbeknownst to me or the NBA, that would let the companies out of the deal any time they wanted.

Like King David, I had no idea any of this was happening. But it didn't stop the NBA and David Stern from punishing me and the entire franchise. The league fined us $8 million for the misrepresentations, which it took out of the TV money we split with all the other NBA franchises. It was a tough pill to swallow.

That was the impetus I needed to realize my partnership with Ray wasn't working. With moral and financial support from the NBA, I began the process to buy out Ray so I could once again run the team without interference.

I was making a new start of things in my personal life as well. I started seeing a woman named Denise, whom I'd met in Charlotte after Carolyn and I divorced. When I told her I was moving the team to New Orleans, she said she was coming with me.

We brought an impressive basketball team to New Orleans as well. We had a talented guard in Baron Davis and a veteran forward in Jamal Mashburn. Plus, head coach Paul Silas had made the move with us to give some continuity. As the first season started in the arena in downtown New Orleans, I felt good about where I was personally and professionally, and I knew I needed to work on improving my life spiritually.

Especially now, because I hoped God would bless our team!

Our first game as the New Orleans Hornets was, ironically, against the last team to play professional basketball in New Orleans. The New Orleans Jazz had left for Utah in 1979, and no regular season NBA game had been held in the city until that night.

On October 30, 2002, the Utah Jazz came back to town, including future Hall of Famers John Stockton and Karl Malone. We had a full house and, like our first game in Charlotte, the citizens of the Crescent City showed an encouraging, consistent level of enthusiasm. They cheered the whole game.

Well, almost the whole game. When the Utah Jazz players came out, our fans loudly booed the team that left them twenty-three years ago.

To commemorate the return of the previous franchise and to help merge the past with the present, we retired the jersey of the old team's best player, "Pistol" Pete Maravich, at halftime. We put his name and old number on our new jerseys with the Hornets logo, though with the old Jazz colors. I couldn't help but remember the time he called me, asking to be our first coach in Charlotte, and thinking about the symmetry now. The crowd went crazy. We ended up winning the game by twenty-five. It was a great night.

We had a good season on the court, winning forty-seven games and making the playoffs. Maintaining that success over the next several seasons, however, proved difficult. Our record bottomed out during the 2004–2005 season, when we won a franchise-low eighteen games. The good news is that our poor performance got us a good draft pick in the NBA lottery.

Going into the 2005–2006 season, we were optimistic about our chances to return to the playoffs. We drafted Chris Paul, a phenomenal guard from Wake Forest, with the third overall pick in the draft. Like another point guard we had in Charlotte from Wake Forest, Muggsy Bogues, Chris was a pest on defense and an excellent passer—but he was a much better scorer than Muggsy. With Chris on board, I was expecting the 2005–2006 season to be very different from the one before it.

I had no idea how different it would be.

In late August 2005, we started to see signs that a hurricane was forming, one that could make its way into the Gulf and possibly impact people in the New Orleans community.

Of course, we now know exactly what Hurricane Katrina would become: One of the most devastating storms in American history. Our new hometown of New Orleans would forever be impacted by the damage it would inflict.

As the storm grew closer, many in the community were overwhelmed with fear. Coming from the middle part of North Carolina, I didn't have a lot of experience with hurricanes. It was surreal to watch TV and see this giant swirling vortex bringing an unknown amount of destruction and chaos and to think that at some point, it could go from different colors on a screen to something flying through your window.

We were put on high alert when Katrina was upgraded to a Category 5 hurricane, the biggest and most destructive.

On August 28, New Orleans mayor Ray Nagin announced a mandatory evacuation of the city for the first time in history. In his press conference ordering the evacuation, Mayor Nagin warned that the storm surge would most likely topple the city's levee system.

That, of course, is exactly what happened.

I had just bought a little country retreat up in Tennessee. Since it was the NBA's offseason, I evacuated there with loved ones as the storm drew near. But of course, New Orleans was always on our mind. That storm was a national story. Everywhere you went, televisions were on, broadcasting pictures of the impact. I could see it headed straight toward our new hometown. Still, we were hopeful. *Maybe it won't be that bad*, we thought. We were hoping for the best but also fearing for the worst.

We underestimated what *worst* could look like. The hurricane was beyond our darkest nightmares.

The levees broke overnight, and water poured into the city's Ninth Ward, flooding one of its most iconic populated areas. The flooding also paralyzed any local or federal government emergency response. The result wasn't just tragic; it was scandalous. People died from drowning, starvation, and dehydration, or they became victims in the surge of lawlessness that followed in the storm's aftermath.

I have since heard stories of people who didn't have the means to evacuate, so they stayed in their houses, which were flooded after the levees broke. One man told me, "I would have been trapped up against the ceiling if I had waited, so I left everything with only a flashlight. Then, I dropped the light, and I was in the water, with it just rising above me. I could feel snakes brushing by me in the water in my own house. It was awful."

I couldn't imagine.

"Eventually, the water pushed me along in the darkness," he continued. "I was just reaching out for anything I could find. I eventually found a branch, which turned out to be connected to a tree."

Imagine being in your home one minute and then hanging on to a tree branch for your life the next.

That's what happened to the people of New Orleans.

The city set up medical operations inside our arena, where doctors and nurses worked around the clock to treat emergencies.

There were *a lot* of emergencies.

I returned after a few days, joined by David Stern and other NBA representatives to tour the damage and assess our new reality. We left the airport and drove out to the Ninth Ward to see firsthand just how bad things were.

It looked like a war zone. Property wasn't just destroyed; it had exploded across an entire block. The smell of death hung in the air. We heard a siren go off as we toured the area, which we soon came to learn meant another body had been discovered.

Being confronted with the traumatic reality of the devastation made me physically ill. But it also made me resolute.

In a weird way, I felt the presence of God. It was a reminder about the immense, infinite, and unquestioned power of God.

You don't have to love the things God puts into your life. I don't love all the things He has put into mine. But, over time, I have come to see even the hard things as opportunities to realize a plan God has for you. I didn't want to lose my father when I was only eight, but that loss shaped the path that led me where I am now. I didn't want to be dealing with the first city in professional sports history to be so shattered by a natural disaster that it would cost state and national emergency response leaders their jobs, but here I was. If this is what God had for me, I would trust there was a reason for it.

The one thing I felt God saying to me throughout that season was, "I have you there for a reason. Be a blessing to this community."

I tried to be a blessing in whatever way I could.

The response from local, state, and national governments was so poor in the aftermath of the storm that many believed New Orleans and her businesses would never recover. Many people I knew who dearly loved New Orleans were talking about leaving. The overall spirit in the city was negative, at least for a while. I heard that Ruth's Chris was moving their main headquarters from New Orleans, primarily because of the storm and the possibilities of more hurricanes in the future. As a businessman who relies on the support of other businesses, that was obviously a troubling sign. But I was committed to being part of the solution. I wasn't going anywhere if I could help it.

David Stern called me every day, asking, "George, how are things going down there?"

"Well, David," I said, "we are trying our best. We are working with the government, trying to be as helpful as we can. But I'm happy to hear any suggestions you have."

"Honestly, George, everything we hear is that you are doing a great job. Just keep it up," he replied.

I appreciated the encouragement. There was so much to do. The situation was literally unprecedented. The NBA had never experienced anything like it before; in fact, nothing like it had ever happened in the history of professional sports.

We were working hard to care for our community first and foremost. But we also had to figure out how to have a professional basketball season when our city clearly couldn't host games for the foreseeable future. Our arena itself was mostly in good shape aside from flooding in the lower levels, but the surrounding area was totally flooded. Even if the surrounding area had been okay, though, no one wanted to take the resources needed to play games away from a community that was dealing with much more serious things than people putting a ball through a hoop.

David and I were convinced that the Hornets had a role to play in helping New Orleans recover and rebuild. More than that, I was convinced God had put me in New Orleans for a reason. I was there to help. I was there to serve.

I knew it wouldn't be easy. Like Peter walking toward Jesus on the stormy waters, I needed to keep my eyes on His power and glory the entire time. I knew there would be moments of frustration and doubt, but I was also hopeful of where this journey would take New Orleans, the Hornets, and me. Walking through "the valley of the shadow of death" (Psalm 23:4 ESV) often becomes the best opportunity to marvel at the places God will carry you if you trust Him enough to follow.

The storm had made a giant valley in New Orleans. All we could do now was walk through it.

"Okay, God," I prayed. "You lead. I'll follow."

Even though I had no idea where He was taking us.

CHAPTER 18

A Different Kind of Rebuilding Year

I've talked before about the story of Joseph in the Bible and how he was an incredible example of God's sovereignty. No matter what happened to Joseph—even when his brothers sold him into slavery and when he was wrongfully imprisoned—God protected him. God allowed Joseph to survive—and to serve.

Joseph's godliness helped him stand out even as a slave, and it put him in a position to serve Potiphar, Pharaoh's top assistant. In prison, Joseph served his fellow prisoners and eventually Pharaoh himself.

I think a lot about the faith it took for Joseph to let God use him that way.

Joseph didn't understand why God allowed him to be sold into slavery and then into prison. But he continued to trust God. In doing so, Joseph saw his story move forward in a way that revealed God's ultimate plan. If Joseph's story ended with his brothers throwing him into the cistern, that would be one thing. But it didn't end there. That cistern eventually transported him to a place where he would serve not only an entire kingdom but also his brothers who had sold him into slavery in the first place. Joseph's brothers' sin took him to the place where he would ultimately save their very lives during the famine.

That's how radical God's grace and heart for redemption is. It was true for Joseph's brothers, and it's still true for all of us now.

As we did our best to lead the basketball team through unprecedented challenges, I was trusting God to put us, like Joseph, in a position to bless and serve whatever community He brought us into.

Discerning where God wanted us to go would take more than faith. It would take wisdom. And it would take work.

Wisdom was accepting the hard reality that we would help New Orleans the most by playing our games elsewhere for the next few months. That was the feedback we consistently got from leaders at every level of government.

The work was figuring out where we could go.

One consequence of the NBA never having dealt with a situation like this before was they didn't have any guidance for us. It was up to us to figure it out for ourselves.

So, I got on the phone to see what I could work out.

Initially, I wanted to play games a couple of hours away in Baton Rouge, the capital of Louisiana. It had two arenas I thought could work, but the damage from Katrina wasn't restricted just to New Orleans. It literally had destroyed homes, lives, and communities across the entire Gulf region. The arenas in Baton Rouge were also being used for relief operations. That basically ruled out any other places in the state.

After that, we considered several cities outside the footprint of Katrina that offered to host us for as long as we needed. The people at NBA headquarters suggested that of all the options, which also included Nashville, Louisville, and San Diego, the Oklahoma City market made the most sense. It was like Charlotte, they told me, in that there was no other professional franchise there. We knew the fans there would be supportive.

I have to admit, I was leery. I didn't know much about Oklahoma City, and it was located in a part of the country I wasn't all that familiar with. Plus, I was from the South, so I was unsure of going to a different part of the country. I don't think I ever got over the stinging "country boy" insults I received decades earlier in California.

I then realized I was acting the same way about Oklahoma City that so many people had acted about Charlotte when we were trying to bring a team there.

It had worked out then. I trusted God that it would work out this time.

We agreed to play thirty-five games in Oklahoma City that season. We also played six in Baton Rouge to maintain at least some presence in Louisiana. The engineers and city officials from New Orleans also told us, depending on how things went, we could even potentially play games back home by the spring.

That was encouraging news, and the players and coaches seemed set to make the best of a tough situation when we started playing in Oklahoma City that November.

In October, our team, staff, ownership, and other key personnel packed up and moved to a third city in five years. Some of our players like P. J. Brown had been with us in Charlotte, and I was always appreciative for the sacrifices they made. They had already moved from Charlotte to New Orleans for us, and now circumstances outside their control were forcing them to move again. The same was true for many of those affiliated with our franchise.

I couldn't help but think about Moses leading the Israelites through the desert. It was hard not to wonder where we were going . . . and if it would all be worth it when we got there.

And then we got to Oklahoma City. It felt like the promised land.

Our first game was like a carnival. They had parties outside the arena, concerts in the streets, and joy in their hearts. I have to say, it was quite the contrast coming from storm-ravaged New Orleans. We hadn't planned on going to OKC, but if we were going to be there, we were going to make the best of it.

We changed our logo slightly, adding "Oklahoma City" underneath our New Orleans Hornets logo. Our jerseys said "Hornets" while we played in the Ford Center arena, but we had a patch on the jerseys that read "OKC."

We were officially branded the New Orleans / Oklahoma City Hornets for that season. I told our players and team we had to go out and make both cities proud. That first game, we sure did.

We played the Sacramento Kings, who were, at the time, a regular playoff team and title contender. But, like our first game in New Orleans, we rode the unbelievable energy from the crowd and jumped out to a big lead we never lost. We beat the Kings by twenty-six.

After the game, I told reporters how impressed I was with the Oklahoma City fans and the community at large.

"When we go back to New Orleans, this city will get a franchise, I'm convinced," I told the reporters. "Whether the NBA is smart enough to come here, or the NHL, or the NFL, or baseball, somebody will come here. This market is going to be too good for them to pass up."

I was right. Oklahoma City was a great home for a professional sports franchise—in the NBA, no less. The success of the Oklahoma City Thunder has shown that to be true.

But Oklahoma City wasn't our home. Our games were there, but my mind and heart were on the community back in New Orleans. We were still in touch with relief workers and the government in charge of the recovery. We offered help in whatever way we could. When we got word that the area around our arena was clear and the community needed less support from emergency services, we started to picture what a return could look like.

We were thrilled to come back to Louisiana for the few games we played in Baton Rouge that season, but we knew the real test was coming back to our city.

That homecoming took place on March 8, 2006, when we played the first professional sports game in New Orleans since Katrina had devastated our home.

I was excited for the chance to bring some sense of normalcy and maybe even healing for our fans and New Orleans residents in general, but I was also nervous. Six months after the storm had passed, less than 190,000 of the city's 465,000 residents had returned. We weren't sure how important something like a basketball game would be, especially after the people had lived through such a tragedy.

Our community showed us just how big of a role the Hornets would play in New Orleans' return from the darkness.

We didn't just sell out the arena; we had a line around the block to get in and ended up selling standing-room-only tickets. Governor Kathleen Blanco was there, and she told me how appreciative she was that we could bring the team back as soon as we did.

"This is incredibly important," Governor Blanco told reporters later. "It's not just a game. It's a real symbol of our ability to restore and renew ourselves and come back strong."

We lost to Kobe Bryant and the Lakers, but—just like my first-ever game as an owner in Charlotte—I didn't care about the score. The fact that we played the game in the first place meant that we won. Helping people who had dealt with unfathomable loss to feel joy and hope again was the biggest victory in the world.

As I drove home after the game, I reflected on the journey God had led me on over the past six months. He gave me a flood to deal with. He gave me players and friends and families dealing with loss to care for. He gave me an entire organization to move on short notice to an unknown place. Then, He brought me back home—and there was no question that New Orleans was now home.

We played the 2006–2007 season in Oklahoma City as well, and we continued to be embraced by the community. But we always planned on returning to New Orleans full time for the following season. Always.

Rumors swirled that we would use the storm and devastation as an excuse to move the team. New Orleans was still really struggling, and there were real questions about what the financial capacity would be moving forward. Half of our season ticket holders had left town, and it wasn't clear they would be returning.

I thought and prayed about this constantly, but I knew we had both an opportunity and responsibility to be at the forefront of rebuilding and promoting New Orleans. People thought I was crazy for wanting to come back. I was criticized heavily by some of my business associates, and even some NBA associates, for making the decision to stay in New Orleans.

There was talk that the New Orleans Saints, who had played some football games in San Antonio, would stay there. That became even more of a reason for me to come back to New Orleans. I felt like if we made the commitment, others would follow. It became as much of a heart move for me as anything else. I knew what the storm had cost me personally and financially. In the years since we had been there, we'd met many other people who loved New Orleans and had deep roots there. We knew how bad they were hurting. I couldn't add to their misery by keeping the Hornets in Oklahoma City.

I prayed hard and felt that it was God's plan for me to bring the team back to New Orleans. That was the main motivation driving me through all of this, but it wasn't easy.

I've never had to deal with so many challenges as I did in the fall of 2007 while we got ready to begin our first season back in New Orleans full time. We had players who didn't want to re-sign because of concerns for their families and the community they would have to live in. We had sponsors and fans who didn't have the resources to help. At times, I even had my own fears and doubts. I was scared to death. All this pressure impacted my health, which I had always taken pride in.

I would not have made it if not for my faith. I was praying to God every day in the lead-up to our first game back in New Orleans. I saw too many indicators of trouble to give me any sense of peace or calm. I just had to trust that God had led us back for a reason.

Our first game back in New Orleans for the next season didn't do much to alleviate my fears. The arena was only half-filled. This wasn't just disappointing; it was embarrassing for me and the NBA. It was also confusing. We had gotten so much support in the few games we played back in New Orleans right after the storm, but now that a post-Katrina reality was settling in, there was real concern. All I could do was pray to God even more.

"God, I feel like You want us to be here," I said. "Please give me the reassurance to know we are here as part of Your plan. We want to bless this community in Your name. Please guide our steps so that Your will is done and this city is restored in a way that glorifies You."

In time, the prayers of our city, the prayers of people who asked God to do a mighty work of restoration, were rewarded. And God would indeed be glorified.

It took some time, but the people of New Orleans returned to the arena. It probably didn't hurt that our team was really good. I also think having the Hornets back helped provide a sense of normalcy to the community. The team had been here before Katrina. Yes, we were gone in the aftermath. But we were back now. Maybe New Orleans was too.

Our fans weren't the only ones who showed up though. Our players did too. They got out in the community, helping wherever and whenever they could. In doing so, they invested in their city and in each other. They were working together off the court, through community appearances and local service projects, and these efforts helped the cooperation on the court. Our community was coming back, and our team was winning.

As we approached the halfway point of the season, we had a real chance to showcase just how much progress New Orleans had made. As part of its plan to support the community, the NBA awarded the 2008 All-Star Game to us. This meant a lot of attention and a lot of support. We'd been working all season to make sure the community put its best foot forward. I thought it would be such a blessing for the entire NBA—but not everyone was convinced it was a good idea.

At the time, only a third of the city's population had returned. Parts of the city were still in ruins.

Billy Hunter, the head of the NBA players' union, threatened to file a lawsuit to stop the game from being played. He was worried that, given the lack of resources and other security concerns, the large crowds might pose a threat to player safety.

Even some of the players didn't think it was a good idea. Tracy McGrady, for example, who was one of the biggest stars in the league, said that playing the game in New Orleans would be more harmful than beneficial. He said the city needed to focus on getting back on its feet instead of hosting the All-Star Game.

But David Stern had promised to help. Our community needed it.

On the third weekend of February 2008, the entire NBA world descended on New Orleans. The year before, the NBA All-Star Game hosted in Las Vegas was marred by numerous arrests and other embarrassing events due to the overcrowding of the city. This year would be different. The NBA came to New Orleans to party, sure. But the NBA also came to help.

The Friday before the All-Star weekend officially began, players, owners, reporters, and even commissioner David Stern took part in the first-ever "NBA Day of Service" event. LeBron James was cleaning windows on a house in the Ninth Ward and helped refurbish basketball courts in the area. Steve Nash and Jason Kidd painted the door on an abandoned home downtown that still hadn't been repaired. Stern painted walls inside a community center.

Hurricane Katrina caused unprecedented destruction to New Orleans and its community. In its own way, the NBA's response was also unprecedented. All told, with Stern's leadership and our team's help, the NBA executed the largest day of community service in the history of professional sports. We had twenty-five hundred people serving in ten different locations, including NBA employees and many members of the Hornets staff. We also had the help of some of the league's top sponsors, investors, and many Louisiana politicians.

The whole weekend couldn't have gone any better. Dwight Howard of the Orlando Magic won the slam dunk contest by putting on a Superman cape and soaring through the air. The All-Star Game itself on Sunday was a competitive contest.

But after the game was over, no one was talking about the score. Years later, when asked about that weekend, LeBron James said that he didn't remember much from the game. He just remembered working in the community. The NBA would remember too.

The 2008 All-Star Game might have brought about the first NBA Day of Service event, but it wasn't the last. The NBA has continued that tradition for every All-Star weekend since.

That weekend really set the course for the rest of our team's season and New Orleans' future. Our team would have its best-ever record, and we came within one game of reaching the Western Conference finals.

The city proved it could be back in the business of hosting major events. That was the first major sporting event in the city since Katrina, and it wouldn't be the last. I felt good about the journey God had led us on. We left amid tragedy but returned, with God's help, as a blessing.

It was the craziest and most challenging journey of my life. And it had taken a toll on me in ways I had not yet fully realized.

CHAPTER 19
Starting a New Season

I've always believed the wisdom in the Bible is for practical application, not just for theoretical understanding. I think that sometimes the seasons of life that cause us the most stress emotionally and mentally can also do the most harm physically. It's one reason I went to the doctor before my trial, just to make sure all my worrying and concern hadn't caused me to develop cancer or any other affliction.

In his letter to the church of Philippi, Paul wrote that we should "not be anxious about anything, but in every situation, by prayer and petition, with thanksgiving, present your requests to God" (Philippians 4:6).

The real wisdom in that passage is that our bodies aren't necessarily meant to carry things like stress at a high level on their own. We are meant to share it with our community, which God designed to help us carry our burdens, and with God Himself.

Having just gone through the season of unimaginable stress that Katrina, the subsequent forced relocation, and eventual return entailed, I was worried that I had internalized more stress than my body could bear. A trip to the doctor's office in 2009 told me I was right.

"I'm sorry, Mr. Shinn, but you have prostate cancer," Dr. Sam Bhayani told me. He was nice enough about it, but I also felt a sense of shame. If I had gotten a biopsy done a long time earlier, he told me, I could have possibly prevented this from happening. I had put it off for several reasons: I had read a book years ago saying biopsies were dangerous; I'd always felt like I was in good health; and I had been so busy dealing with the Hornets and all the issues related to their location that I honestly never made the time.

That had been a mistake.

Dr. Bhayani told me my cancer was aggressive but treatable. After consulting with Dr. Patrick Walsh, a surgeon and foremost expert on prostate cancer, I was told I would have to wait ninety days for the biopsy wound to heal before surgeons could remove the cancer. In the meantime, I was told not to eat anything with sugar in it, because that could feed the cancer.

I spent the next ninety days walking, praying, and not eating sugar. But I wasn't just waiting around. I got aggressive with treating my cancer holistically to help prevent the cancer's aggressive growth. I went to Hippocrates Wellness facility in West Palm Beach, which specialized in helping people with medical issues get healthier. It helped me stick to the dietary and lifestyle regimen that would keep my prostate cancer from spreading.

It worked. I dropped forty pounds by the time my surgery date rolled around. When I got the call that the surgery had been a success and I was cancer-free, I fell to my knees and literally cried out in thanks to God. Once again, He had delivered me from potential tragedy. And, once again, I had an opportunity to redirect my efforts on this earth to point people toward life beyond it.

Recovering from cancer changed me in a way I hadn't anticipated. I had dealt with medical issues before and have had to reconcile the impact my career was having on my health. The fact that I had a stroke on the day of Charlotte's first-ever win wasn't lost on me. When I recovered after the stroke, I couldn't wait to get back to the office. I even went back before they told me I should, and I stayed longer than they told me I could.

Now, though, things seemed different. I felt like God was telling me it was okay to loosen my grip. For the first time, I felt like He was telling me there were other things in His plan I needed to do. Maybe part of it was the fact that I had gotten prostate cancer. Now that I realized how important early detection and awareness was, I became passionate about letting other people know. But there was more to it than that.

I felt like I had a new lease on life, along with the energy to be a blessing to the New Orleans community and beyond. I knew that, if I was going to stay healthy, I needed to take steps to reduce as much stress in my life as possible. Unfortunately, that meant giving up my ownership of the New Orleans Hornets.

I had done my best to make things work financially amid incredibly difficult financial circumstances. But the reality is that the storm and subsequent years of forced relocation, playing in numerous cities, rebuilding efforts and investment, and operating in a market struggling with the biggest natural disaster in the last century took a financial toll.

All that stress had given my body cancer. What do you think it did to my wallet?

Still, I had made a promise to the city of New Orleans, and I made a promise to God. I was committed to keeping the team in the city and I would do that, no matter what it took.

Once he found out I was interested in selling the team, Bay Area businessman Larry Ellison approached me with an offer of $350 million. That sounded more than fair to me, but he wanted to move the team to the West Coast. That was a nonstarter.

Saints owner Tom Benson approached me too, but we couldn't agree on a price. My minority owner, Gary Chouest, also considered buying the team, which would have been great. Gary was one of the most humble, kind, and savvy businessmen I knew. He was an excellent partner, but he ultimately decided he didn't have the expertise to buy the team.

I was frustrated with some of the challenges selling the team presented, but I was not deterred. I'd never been afraid to think of creative solutions to problems before. So, I called David Stern with an idea.

"You want to keep the team in New Orleans, and so do I," I told him. "For whatever reason, we don't have anyone who can buy the team right now that fits the profile of what we both are looking for. But . . . what if *you* bought the team from me?"

Stern said he was intrigued, and he liked the idea of taking an unprecedented step to keep the team in the area. After all, David had put his name and reputation on the line by not only having the All-Star Game there in 2008 but by committing so many NBA resources to the area to help with the rebuild.

The NBA agreed to the arrangement, and I agreed to take less than what Larry Ellison had offered me for the team. In May 2010, I sold the Hornets back to the NBA for $325 million. Later, the NBA sold the team to Tom Benson for $350 million, ensuring the team would stay in New Orleans for the foreseeable future. I was proud of how it all had worked out. I got a fair price, the NBA made $25 million, and Tom Benson got the team for a fair price.

It's a weird feeling, selling a professional sports team. I had been the owner for almost twenty-five years, more than a third of my life. That was longer than I had owned or run any other business and almost as long as I was married. Selling the team had its advantages, sure. But it also meant I wasn't part of the NBA club anymore.

After a quarter of a century being around people at that level, it sort of became part of my identity—not that I needed the celebrity association to feel good about myself. I was proud of my legacy as an NBA owner. I brought professional basketball for the first time to Charlotte, New Orleans, and even Oklahoma City, who, incidentally, got their own team shortly after we moved out. Since Charlotte was awarded another expansion team after we left for New Orleans, I took pride in operating teams in three different cities and markets that are still current homes to NBA teams. As several reporters have noted, ten percent of the NBA teams in the league today are around because our organization brought basketball to those cities. Still, it was hard not to be a little sad and nostalgic about the contributions I had made to the NBA—and the contributions it had made to me.

But I also had 325 million reasons to move on. And God had bigger plans for me.

Even before I had any real money, I had been into cars. Ever since I helped my father by washing them in his garage, I'd been in love with sleek, fast, and classic cars. My passion for buying and collecting cars grew in relation to my bank account. After all, I met Rick Hendrick because I was always interested in new and sometimes exotic vehicles.

I now had a collection of more than seventy cars, including the car used in the movie *Bonnie and Clyde*. I also had a few different types of '57 Chevrolets, which had always been my favorite car.

Now that I had a significant amount of money burning a hole in my pocket, I was ready to continue to pursue that passion. I went to an auction shortly after receiving a big check from the NBA and bought $3 million worth of cars.

I never said it wasn't an expensive hobby.

I don't know if it was because of my newfound health, or the removal of stress from the challenges the NBA had brought over the past few years, or the fact that God continued to bless me financially in ways I never could have imagined, but I also set out to invest in real estate in a way I hadn't before. That meant buying and selling homes in a number of places, including Florida, Tennessee, North Carolina, and Louisiana. While part of it was something to keep my business senses intact and part of it was fun, it was also impactful personally. And not in a positive way.

All the changes had an impact on my marriage So, after sixteen years, Denise and I agreed to separate. Getting a divorce for a second time was not easy, but the circumstances this time couldn't have been more different from the first. Our visions for what our future would be, though, were just too different, and we couldn't work through it.

At this point, I was in my seventies, single again, and financially set for life. But I'd learned my lessons about what happens when you make poor decisions. My wealth was a blessing from God, and I was determined to be a good steward of it. Plus, since I wasn't a husband or an NBA owner anymore, I had more space in my life for God to give me a new identity. So, with the help of trusted spiritual advisers, I started investing more seriously than ever before in philanthropy.

Jesus once famously told a young man, whom the Bible tells us had great wealth, that "if you want to be perfect, go, sell your possessions and give to the poor" (Matthew 19:21).

When the young man heard this, the Gospel of Matthew continues, "he went away sad, because he had great wealth" (verse 22).

Jesus then said one of the most famous lines in the Bible. "It is easier for a camel to go through the eye of a needle than for someone who is rich to enter the kingdom of God," Jesus said before reminding us, "With God all things are possible" verses 23, 26).

I have failed in the past at fleeing from and resisting temptation. I now realize God has blessed me with resources that once again might lead me down the wrong path. But I know that with God, all things are possible. He is the reason I have been given the chance to use the resources He has given me to make His name known and to help glorify Him. So, I still get up every day and say, "Good morning, God." And even though I sold my basketball team, I get up every morning knowing I have work to do.

I'm spending the rest of my life focusing on God, and I'm trusting Him to lead my steps and use the resources He has provided to make His name known on earth.

Through my foundation, I've been blessed to learn about and contribute toward a variety of causes, everything from medical centers in Haiti to adoption agencies in Tennessee to churches all throughout the country.

The Bible 's very clear about who Jesus cared for and who He chose not to associate with. He regularly corrected the Pharisees, the religious elite of that time, and went out of

His way to love sinners and people with physical disabilities. During His ministry on earth, Jesus helped the lame walk, the blind see, and used the power of the Most High to help the least of these.

That became my focus. God had blessed me with a fortune. Now I wanted to bless those without one. I spent the next few years of my life focused not on building a kingdom on earth but on storing treasure in heaven.

Then God sent an angel to help me.

One day, through mutual friends, I met a woman named Megan. She was significantly younger than me, so at first I wasn't sure if it could turn into an actual relationship. But the more we spoke and got to know each other, the more I saw that, while we did have an age difference, her heart for God was timeless. We had a lot of other common interests, including traveling and animals. But mostly, she was on fire to love others like Jesus.

Megan is beautiful, but her love for the Lord, her ability to find joy in the smallest moments of everyday life, and her desire to use the strengths God gave her to care for others is what truly took my breath away. She loves things incredibly well, and I thank God every day for giving me someone to love me in a way that reminds me of the way I know God loves all of us.

We were married on June 14, 2020, in the red-roof barn of our Franklin, Tennessee, ranch. Our two dogs rode in the cab with us in my 1949 Chevrolet truck as we rode off into the sunset.

But our story with God was hardly over.

One day, Megan woke up in the middle of the night and felt like she was hearing something from God. She shook me so hard I couldn't help but wake up.

"George," she said softly. "We need to do something to help the people in Ukraine."

Megan's heart for God is unquestionably pure. But if she is waking me up in the middle of the night, I want to do what she says—both because I believe she is hearing from God . . . and because I'd like to go back to sleep.

When we got up a few hours later, Megan and I decided to donate a car from my collection, a 2009 Ford Shelby GT500 Super Snake, to an upcoming Barrett-Jackson car auction, in which all the proceeds would go toward relief work being done in and for Ukraine by Samaritan's Purse. Florida governor Ron DeSantis acted as the emcee, and our car was part of a package of two collector vehicles.

The bids kept climbing, and the auctioneer finally said "sold" at the total of $1 million.

I thought we could do more.

I pledged a $100,000 donation on top of the $1 million the car had just earned, and I challenged the crowd to match it. One by one, another six people matched my pledge. After another donation and a literal passing of the hat in the crowd that day, we raised a total of $1.76 million for the victims of the Russian invasion into Ukraine.

Megan and I couldn't believe it. It was more than we ever imagined we might be able to bring in. I asked Steve Davis, the president of Barrett-Jackson, "Who in the world paid one million dollars for this car?"

Steve just looked back at me. "Rick Hendrick," he said matter-of-factly.

When I heard that, I started bawling. I couldn't believe that my business partner, the man I helped launch his first auto dealership decades ago, was the winning bidder.

Everywhere I looked, in that moment, I saw God.

I saw Him in my father, whose love for cars inspired me to start collecting them in the first place. I have a replica of the service station he worked at in our car barn at my Tennessee ranch. And now I use that car barn, and all the cars I've been blessed to acquire, to help those in need by holding fundraising events for charity.

I saw Him in my friendship with Rick, who is just one of the many people who have been instrumental in getting me where I am today.

I saw Him in Megan, who had the idea to do something for the people of Ukraine.

I saw Him in the generosity of the crowd, who collectively gave more than I ever imagined. I am blown away by the way God brings all the pieces of our lives together to paint a picture that points back to Him.

I can't tell you how overwhelming it is to think about how God has used all of them—and all of my life—to bring together what happened in that car auction. It is also overwhelming to think about what continues to happen through all the amazing ways God works in my life.

That's my story right now. That's where my journey has taken me.

I'm grateful for the road God has allowed me to travel, bumps and all. Those rough parts helped me straighten up and ultimately brought me to where I am today. As I walk past the trucks, roadsters, and coupes in my barn, I think about all the lives these cars can now bless. Those thoughts make me grateful for my past and make me excited for the parts of my journey still to come.

Now, even in my eighties, I still need to work on remembering who really is behind the wheel.

CHAPTER 20

Finding My True Purpose

As I've noted, one of the people in the Bible I can relate to the most is David. Like me, he was short. And, like me, he had his share of personal failures. But David didn't let that stop him from repenting, pursuing God, and allowing the Lord to use him in ways that glorified God and helped further His kingdom.

But I can also relate to and am drawn to the story of Moses. Partly because of how his mother sacrificed so much to give Moses a better life, I see myself in his story as well. Like Moses, I came from a humble beginning, only to have God elevate me to a position of leadership and influence.

Moses led the Israelites through the desert and finally into the promised land. Obviously, I didn't do anything like that; I just brought a basketball team to my home state. But I think doing that helped change lives. And, like Moses, I felt unprepared and ill-equipped to do it. But just as Moses was given Aaron to help him and a staff to summon the Lord's strength, I was given some amazing people to help make our impossible dream come true.

But that's not the only way I feel like Moses.

On reaching the precipice of the destiny the Lord called him to, Moses got distracted by his own pride. In the book of Numbers, we learn that, after leading the Israelites through so many incredible moments, including the parting of the Red Sea and being fed by manna from heaven, Moses eventually took God's presence and provision for granted.

When the people Moses was leading were thirsty, they complained to him.

"Why did you bring the Lord's community into this wilderness, that we and our livestock should die here? Why did you bring us up out of Egypt to this terrible place?" (Numbers 20:4–5).

Even after being faithfully led by Moses and kept alive by God for forty years, the Israelites were saying it would have been better for them to still be in Egypt, where they were slaves for Pharaoh.

Moses and Aaron asked God for guidance. God told Moses to gather everyone together and "speak to that rock before their eyes and it will pour out its water" (Numbers 20:8).

God wasn't troubled by the people's impatience. God wanted Moses, by speaking to the rock in front of everyone, to once again remind them about the central role He plays in providing all things for His people.

But this time Moses got impatient. After assembling the Israelites, Moses said to God's people, "Listen, you rebels, must we bring you water out of this rock?" (Numbers 20:10). Then he struck the rock twice with his staff. The rock produced water. But it wasn't the outcome that mattered. It was the process.

Moses used the staff God had given him, the staff that had parted the Red Sea, to do this. But he didn't get the water the way God wanted. He took a tool from God and used it in his own way, not the way God had instructed.

It might seem like a small thing, but the point is, even those we revere as biblical icons are capable of disobedience.

Moses was no different.

God eventually told Moses that he would not be allowed to set foot in the promised land as a result of his behavior, even after forty years of leading His people.

Most people don't realize how the Bible helps us realize how good God is by showing us flaws in the very people He uses to tell His story. Moses, after all, was a murderer. And while he spent years following God and leading His chosen people, even Moses was guilty of not relying on God and taking things into his own hands.

But God still used Moses—and forgave him.

In the biblical account of what is known as the transfiguration, the Gospel of Matthew tells us, "After six days Jesus took with him Peter, James, and John the brother of James, and led them up a high mountain by themselves. There he was transfigured before them. His face shone like the sun, and his clothes became as white as the light. Just then there appeared before them Moses and Elijah, talking with Jesus" (17:1–3).

Even after his disobedience, Moses, who suffered severe consequences, still made it to the eternal promised land—heaven.

I'm certainly not like Moses in terms of my levels of spiritual leadership, but I *can* relate to his story in many other ways.

From an early age, I felt like God had set me apart and took care of me because He knew I was someone who wanted to honor Him. After my moment on the side of I-85, I felt God's presence and provision in the growth and success of my business life. When David Stern called me to say we had been awarded an NBA team, my first words were, "Thank you, Jesus." My intention, with every ounce of my body, was to honor God in the way we ran that team.

Obviously, along the way, I fell short of that goal.

But one thing I've learned in my eighty-plus years on this earth: life isn't about the struggle of this moment; it's about the promise of the next one.

I've learned to never let my eyes focus more on my own shortcomings than on God's perfection. We are called to look and live like Jesus. We might not get it right all the time, but we should never stop trying.

I've come to realize that one of the punishments of sin is sin itself. By definition, choosing something other than the path God chose for you means you are getting less than what He wanted for you. That's what happened to Moses, and that's what happened to me.

Because of the path I chose, one of poor choices and poor judgment, I had to leave the people of Charlotte, the community I loved. That path truly led me on a journey that seemed biblical in its own way.

I have failed and, as a result, lost the respect of my hometown. The next place I went had a flood and saw tremendous loss—but also profound redemption. And while I am grateful for the blessings and experiences of New Orleans and all the other places I've lived, North Carolina will always be home.

That's why I'll always be grateful, even years after leaving Charlotte the way I did, I was able to return to bless the community I came from. It's not exactly Moses making it to the promised land, but North Carolina is the land *I* made a promise to. And I always try and keep my promises.

My life doesn't make sense. There's no reason that someone who was born in Kannapolis, North Carolina, who lost his father at such a young age, should have had the life I've had. God is the only reason for our blessings. It's easy to forget that. Moses forgot it. The Israelites Moses led out of slavery forgot it. And I, too, have forgotten it at times.

But I was lucky enough to remember. We all are. God loves us enough to meet us where we are, but He loves us too much to let us stay there. I wandered from God on occasion, but the thing I want people to remember about me is that I found my way back to Him. Even with all my disobedience, I never forgot who God was. God is bigger than all our failures. He is stronger than our weakness. His perfection is more than enough to make up for our flaws. In fact, God's so good that His plan actually *uses* our flaws for His own good!

The city of Charlotte brought me some of my greatest highs in life. It also brought me some of my greatest lows. Bringing the Hornets to town was one of the greatest moments of my life; and the night we got our first win, I also nearly lost my life. But just as a Charlotte hospital helped save my life when I suffered the same kind of stroke that killed my father, a Charlotte hospital was now how my effort to improve my relationship with the city would begin.

Felix Sabates, one of my partners in the Hornets ownership group and one of the most colorful people I've ever known in my life, reached out a few years ago with an idea. He knew that I hadn't spent much time in Charlotte in recent years and thought he had a way for me to re-engage with the community. Atrium Hospital, which is part of the Carolina Medical Center, was raising money for a new stroke center that would, among other things, create ways to treat stroke victims in rural areas as well as in the city. He suggested I think about making a donation that would jump-start the effort.

"Come on, George. You can donate $10 million, can't you?" he said.

"Let me pray about it, Felix."

I liked the idea of making a donation to something that would benefit the community that had given so much to me. I *really* liked that I'd be giving to something that would actually save lives—lives of stroke victims just like I'd been all those years ago. I also knew in my heart that leading with generosity and humility would be the best way to do it.

But $10 million was a lot of money.

"What about $5 million, Felix?" I asked him. He always did like to negotiate.

"George, don't you realize this hospital saved your life?" he said.

"Yes, I do remember that," I told him.

We decided to meet in the middle, and so, just before the global pandemic turned the world upside down, Megan and I agreed to give a $7.5 million donation to Charlotte's Atrium Health Foundation, in support of the Atrium Health Stroke Network.

Thinking about it now, I can see the beautiful symmetry that comes only from an author like God. The money we were able to donate, which in part came from my sale of the Hornets basketball team, will be used to fund a new stroke center. The stroke that killed my father is what sent me on this journey in the first place, and any success I've had, starting out as the poor son of a single mother and as someone who finished last in his class, is possible only because of God.

I mean, how wild is that?

I have seen how God has blessed me beyond my wildest dreams. He has blessed me with three kids. He has blessed me to find love.

More importantly, He's blessed me with the wisdom to know that bringing professional basketball to North Carolina was not the most important part of my legacy.

In that story from Matthew, after the disciples went with Jesus to the mountaintop and saw God's light shine down on Him, and after Peter, James, and John saw Elijah and Moses, something amazing happened. In fact, the next part of Scripture is among my favorite verses. After they saw the two Old Testament figures in heaven, Matthew 17:5–8 tells us, "While he was still speaking, a bright cloud covered them, and a voice from the cloud said, 'This is my Son, whom I love; with him I am well pleased. Listen to him!' When the disciples heard this, they fell facedown to the ground, terrified. But Jesus came and touched them. 'Get up,' he said. 'Don't be afraid.' When they looked up, they saw no one except Jesus."

That has long been my goal. I hope that, despite my own failings, when my race is run and my time on earth has ended, when people look at my life, they see God's grace. I hope they see someone who has learned, time and again, to try and be obedient and faithful to His will.

That's why I came back to Charlotte. I'm not just giving $7.5 million to a hospital. I'm trying to die to myself in such a way that, when people look at what's left, all they see is God.

We made the donation to the hospital just before COVID shut things down. As a result, we didn't get to tour the hospital for several years. That meant my return to Charlotte was delayed even longer. But that's okay. God's timing is perfect. In the fall of 2022, Megan and I finally got to come back, see the hospital, and reconnect with old friends.

But the work we are committed to doesn't stop with this Charlotte hospital.

Megan and I made the decision that, after my death, all the wealth and resources God has given me will be distributed to the various nonprofits and charitable organizations my foundation now supports. The George Shinn Foundation continues to do amazing things today. We fund homes that help kids in foster care find permanent homes with loving families. We fund a home for girls in Haiti that gives them a chance to break cycles of generational difficulty. We fund a group in Tennessee that helps refugees get settled in a new place and gives them the things they need to start a new and hopefully better life. We donated $1 million to a new building for the Charlotte Rescue Mission, which does amazing work helping people recover from the horrors of addiction. And we help Franklin Graham and his team at Samaritan's Purse to spread the gospel of Jesus Christ all over the world through acts of generosity and humanitarian relief.

The foundation will continue long after I pass, helping equip people to be the hands and feet of the work God has for us while on this earth and to point to our eternal home in heaven. George Shinn won't be around anymore, but the life-changing grace of God and the overwhelming generosity the foundation provides will remain.

It has taken years, and I continue to stumble and struggle every day in my attempts to get it right, but God continues to give us all chances to live faithfully and be obedient to His will.

My name is George. I am a man—a man who is deeply flawed but a man who has learned that God loves me and can use me in spite of, and in some ways *because of*, those flaws.

The biggest mistake you can make when you feel like God might be calling you to serve His kingdom is to focus on your own sins instead of God's grace. God's business model doesn't just tolerate sinners; it requires the sinner to be saved by His grace. If God couldn't use broken people, He wouldn't have anyone to use! God told the apostle Paul, "My grace is sufficient for you, for my power is made perfect in weakness" (2 Corinthians 12:9).

I thank God every day for the way He has used me. And I pray that you, too, will accept His invitation to be used. If you learn anything from my story, it's that God can use anyone and everyone for His good and perfect purpose. If you make the decision to invite God into your life and trust Him to be in charge, you'd better buckle up and get ready for incredible things to happen. Because, while we might be flawed, God is too big to fail.

Acknowledgments

I've written a number of books in my life, but I have to say that writing this one was a process unlike any other. Sharing my personal journey of faith, through the highs and lows of life and the lessons God taught me along the way, has been such a blessing, and I'm so grateful to the people God has put in my life to help me.

First and foremost, I'd like to thank my incredible wife, Megan, whose heart to love God by loving others has been such an inspiration to me. She is gorgeous on the outside, but her beauty on the inside is breathtaking.

Her heart for others has led us, and the George Shinn Foundation, to be able to bless others in their work spreading the gospel of Jesus Christ, and through that effort we have been able to work with Franklin and Edward Graham. I'm so humbled and honored to have been able to see up close what being the hands and feet of Jesus looks like in real life, and I thank them for showing the rest of us what it means to live every day in service to Him.

I'd like to thank my children, whom I love more than anything else on this earth. I have had the opportunity to do many amazing things in this life, but none of them top being their dad.

This book wouldn't be possible without my coauthor, Don Yaeger, and the amazing team at Maxwell Leadership publishing. Don has been an absolute joy to work with, and his talent with the written word is matched only by his love for the Lord.

My journey from the poorest and worst student in my class to unimagined professional success is truly the kind of thing only God could have made happen. But it also wouldn't have been possible without a number of people who helped me along the way.

My mother, Irene Shinn, faced one setback after another, yet never let the hand life dealt her keep her from loving God, and me, every day. My good friend and former business partner Rick Hendrick has been a confidant, advisor, listener, and supporter since the day I met him, and I wouldn't be here today if it weren't for him. The team of people who worked for our original team of George Shinn and Associates helped me have the kind of professional success that made me think bringing a professional sports team to Charlotte was possible in the first place. David Stern, Russ Granik, and Gary Bettman, along with the other NBA executives who took a chance on the country boy with a funny accent from North Carolina, helped make history, and transformed not only a state, but an entire region as well. And finally, the people of Charlotte, who showed so much support and love to the Charlotte Hornets franchise, its players, and the larger community it created, brought me and so many others unimagined joy.

Thanks to all of them for the role they played in allowing me to be led by God to the places He wanted me to go, and thanks to you, the reader, for following along as well.

I hope you found the journey worthwhile. I know I did.